Help, My Marriage Hurts!

Anthology Compiled by Oscar & Crystal Jones

Authors:

Rene & Maria Aguirre, Carleton & Angela Booker, Mark & Sherri Bryant, Greg & Saryta Colbert, Ron & LaShun Franklin, Byron & Gwendolyn Holloway, Oscar & Crystal Jones, Kenneth & Adrienne Nears, Ralph & Lashawnda Williams, Tony & Aries Winans

Help! My Marriage Hurts!

Copyright © 2022 by Oscar & Crystal Jones
All Rights Reserved.

Printed in the U.S.

Edited, formatted, and published by
Destiny House Publishing, LLC.
P.O. Box 19774 Detroit, MI 48219
inquiry@destinyhousepublishing.com
www.destinyhousepublishing.com
404.993.0830

Cover by Kingdom Graphic Designs

This work may not be used in any form, or reproduced by any means, in whole or in part, without written permission from Destiny House Publishing, LLC, Marriage for a Lifetime Ministries, or the authors. Unless otherwise stated, all scripture is from the King James Version (KJV)

ISBN: 978-1-936867-83-7

Table of Contents

Chapter 1
Addictions in the Pews 1

Chapter 2
After An Affair 17

Chapter 3
For Richer or for Poorer: Drowning in Debt 27

Chapter 4
Forsaking All Others: Priority of Marriage 41

Chapter 5
Grief: Ain't Nobody Got Time for That 49

Chapter 6
In Sickness & In Health 65

Chapter 7
Integrating In-laws 81

Chapter 8
Overcoming Pornography by Covenantal Collaboration 95

Chapter 9
Overcommitment: Crowded Out 113

Chapter 10
Tug of War: Power Struggles 119

Chapter 11
Unforgiveness: The Root 131

Chapter 12
Yours, Mine, & Ours: Blending Families 141

INTRODUCTION

How do you stop the pain of a breaking or broken marriage? Can the trajectory of a relationship be shifted from unhealthy to thriving? Is there any hope? We contend that there is.

Marriage was God's idea. He gifted it to us in the earth to properly steward. Unfortunately the evil one hates marriage, because it is a picture of Christ and the church. So when you said, "I do", Satan said, "We'll see." He conspired and is conspiring to sabotage your gift. Know that he is a liar. And he cannot triumph over you unless you throw in the towel. Luke 19:10 says, Behold, I give unto you power to tread on serpents and scorpions, and over all the power of the enemy: and nothing shall by any means hurt you. That's the word that you will need to fight with. God, the Creator of marriage, knew that sin would thrash a beating on you and your relationship. So He sent His Son to die to pay the price for sin. This resulted in our restoration to our relationship with God, the Father. And He has bestowed upon us the ministry of reconciliation. There is no marriage beyond God's power, no matter how desperate it feels.

Forgiveness is the help that God offers us. It's not cheap. It's powerful and life-producing. We can receive it and offer it to our spouses because of who God is in our lives. It's His grace that keeps us going or we all would have been counted out a long time ago.

We (Oscar & Crystal Jones) have gathered the premiere marriage ministry leaders around the country to speak to the issues that crush the hearts of so many. These leaders speak with transparency about their own struggles and how they were able to overcome the traps of the deceitful one. The path of victory is plainly laid out for others to follow.

What does God have to say about your specific struggle with your spouse? If you will just venture in with an open heart, you will hear the Lord speak. He has the answers you need.

You will find that the authors offer concrete truths. We all understand that marriage is not easy. It will take faith and commitment to get to the other side of the pain you face. But it is possible.

It is not necessary to read this book in chronological order. The topics are arranged in alphabetical order to make your subject easy to find. Feel free to go directly to the subject(s) with which you are struggling. There is a prayer and some scriptures at the very end for support.

Whatever you are facing today, know this...you are not alone. The pages you are about to read are written by those who have had the same pain and brokenness. We have shed our own tears and are able to point the way to healing and the Healer who promises to be there with you. God says, He sent His Word and healed His people. Healing awaits you.

We invite you to step boldly into your own healing. Take a deep breath and read on...

ONE
Addictions in the Pews

Tony & Aries Winans

Club 1 Marriage Ministry

Have you ever considered that you may have an addiction? We often overlook small things that capture our attention and drive our responses. When we are addicted, our commitments to these things usually come with excuses to defend their purpose. For example, if you regularly drink coffee every morning and happen to miss your daily routine, finding yourself short tempered and moody, you may respond by saying, "Now, you know I didn't have my coffee, today" as if that one missed cup excuses your actions. Or maybe you were rudely interrupted while playing a game or watching a movie that you really enjoyed, to talk about something *"important"*. Do you respond with the aggravation that you are feeling? We can all become drawn away by something of habit until it evolves into an addiction.

We fight to defend the continuation of the thing we've grown addicted. We ultimately get agitated because our explanation doesn't make sense to others. It will weigh on the marriage if not handled properly. We (Tony & Aries) both had addictions or strongholds that we subjected ourselves to that birthed some disheartening consequences. We will both offer our personal depictions of what we dealt with and how they played out in our marriage.

I'm sure I'm (Tony) not the only one who desires a relief from life every so often. I'm talking about relief from the multiple attitudes at the workplace or the drivers on the road who have the nerve to go the speed limit when traffic is flowing at a faster pace, or when bills are always due on time… you know… life. To manage and exhale from it all, my wife and I put in place a time to decompress from it all. I had an entire hour to play my games on my phone before the transition from work to home. Of course, I could've done something else, but this was my peace, which may be different from others. You may enjoy a workout, a time of just being still or even taking a nap; it all varies depending on the person.

Gradually my time to decompress warranted more than what we agreed; the hour just wasn't enough anymore. I'd ask for one more game or let me finish up this last one or I'd keep playing until I heard, "Baby, what are you doing?" from my wife. My time to relax in my eyes was now viewed as an escape and to be told I had to give it up had now provoked an attitude. The blame shifted to statements like, "You're exaggerating, it's only a game" and "I don't say anything when you have your time". I was making more allowances for my games than for my wife.

Being addicted to what was purposed for a time of relaxation brought turmoil in our marriage. While trying to communicate my point, her perception seemed more judgmental than helpful. I felt attacked. But it was my choices that were playing a part in killing my marriage. So, while feeding this addiction more and more time, I was also starving my wife of attention and neglecting other obligations. My responses to her were short and disengaged. I would exhibit frustration if she asked for my attention or disrupted my game. You would think the covenant was with my device and my wife was trying to "...put us asunder".

After the constant back and forth, a statement my wife made crept through my pride and arrogance. "You spend more time with that game than you do with me!" Even with the disgruntled look on my face while mumbling, "You trippin!" I couldn't help but take notice to what was said. How did I get so caught up in this game to the point of it pulling me away from everything else? What was I hiding from that caused me to shrink into this place of disconnection? I mean the game is enjoyable, but it couldn't be what's driving my decisions. Could it?

Well, I found out the hard way. I hadn't only shut out my wife, but I had also shut out God. My irresponsibility to the obvious chaos surrounding me lead to us being evicted from our home. Cars broke down for failure to keep up the maintenance. Repossessions happened due to our mismanagement of finances. The game, although addictive, was a tool I used to escape my fears. Feelings of hopelessness and helplessness added fuel to the fire and massaged depression into my mind. But I was a functioning addict. I knew how to smile and assure people all was well, while my life was crumbling all around me.

You might be thinking, "That escalated quickly!" You're correct, it doesn't take long for a habit to turn into an addiction. With a habit, you'll have sequences in your life that are hard to give up. However, an addiction leads you to sacrifice any and everything to stay in that cycle. I had to face the hard truth that the decision I needed to make was more than limiting my game time. Faith was the only negotiating factor that could oppose this fear. My good ideas were now bad ideas in the light of God's. I had to realize that the hiding place of my addiction only sheltered my fear of being led by Father God. Once that happened, I had to come out and come under His leading.

I had to acknowledge my fault; but more than that, I had to actively commit to change. A solidified 180 turn was necessary while avoiding the dizziness of 360 spins that only caused me to be unbalanced, then eventually fall. Plainly put, I needed to repent! Confessing the object of my addiction only revealed my fear of leading that had to be dealt with. So, I followed the lead of humility. I immediately cut the games on my phone to face what needed to be faced (cold turkey). I came under accountability to help navigate me through our finances. I listened to God. I listened to my wife. And I listened to my leaders. I fussed and kicked through the process, but the mess of what was behind me was nonnegotiable. I could not return. God proved Romans 8:18 to me, *"For I reckon that the sufferings of this present time are not worthy to be compared with the glory which shall be revealed in us."*.

The reconnection with God uploaded the wisdom that *an identified addiction* is usually the cover for an undealt with sin. **Proverbs 28: 13, He that covereth his sins shall not prosper: but whoso confesseth and forsaketh them shall have mercy.** Understanding this made sense of my defensive behavior when what was housing sin (the addiction) was challenged. Imagine someone constantly banging on the door of your home telling you to come out while you're comfortably positioned. That person will not be met with a calm attitude and kind words. My wife was throwing bricks through the window of my addiction and the unconfessed sin in me was screaming out through broken glass. I allowed the sin to take residence. Until I issued a letter of eviction, the idea of moving was not a thought. But it took steps, I had to follow this order, ***James 4:7 Submit yourselves therefore to God. Resist the devil, and he will flee from you.*** Eviction couldn't come before submission.

I was offending God throughout this entire process and my wife and children were in the sinking ship. Parallel to Jonah, if I had continued running and hiding, the sea of our life would have continued to rage. Thank God for His mercy.

Over the course of our nearly 12 ½ years of marriage, the Lord helped us to see our destructive patterns and nasty addictions. One of my (Aries) issues was (cue dramatic music) - shopping. Yes! My motto coming into the marriage was pretty much, "it's my money and I want it now!" In my single days, I could be found speeding down the street, blasting Shopaholic on my radio while trying to figure out how to get more money, so I could spend more money. Notice I didn't say *make* more because if it could be given, I would gladly take it.

Unfortunately for my soon-to-be husband, I came into the marriage with an unhealthy view of finances. When we got married, both of us continued to work. I was also in school in the early years of our marriage. When the student refund came, I would take every dime and blow it on whatever I wanted. Bills? No. Savings? Who has time for that? Buying a plane ticket to visit my friends in Florida? Now you're talking. But first, let me stop at Starbucks after that, I will order a few new outfits and a couple of pairs of shoes for the trip.

Although I had a habit of reckless spending, I believed that I could stop at any time. Isn't that the thought of all addicts? I believed I could start saving, budgeting, and cut back on my luxuries. However, I wasn't pressed to do it.

The idea of "one pot" within marriage was ok for me. I was excited about working and putting our checks in our bank account. I honored my husband as the head of the household and totally trusted him to manage everything. I mean "everything", especially when it came to paying bills and managing the finances. I wanted no parts of it. So like an ostrich, I put my head in the sand and proceeded to plan my next shopping trip.

Everything was fine until I learned that my honey-bunch sugar plum wasn't taking care of the bills. In fact, he was hiding **all of them** on top of the refrigerator, where I couldn't see them. This was only the beginning. Later, the Lord allowed me to start a small massage business making pretty decent money. I would work at the Grand Prix for one weekend to give massages to the drivers and media personnel, before and after events. I would bring home a few thousand dollars which my husband would take all of it and use it on the bills. I felt robbed. Hurt. I felt like I couldn't trust him with the business money. So in turn, I gave in and spent whatever I wanted, as well. I figured if he's going to take it, I might, as well, get what I can first. This also caused me to not be as open with how much money I made that day, for fear he would say he needed it to pay a bill.

As time progressed, my spending didn't get any better. I became an emotional spender. I shopped when I was happy, frustrated, bored, angry, and of course - when I felt like I needed a reward. Shopping was the answer! There were times, I would go shopping for absolutely no reason at all. Just because it felt good to take my mind off of responsibilities, pressures, stress, and more.

Even if I wasn't shopping for myself. I would shop the clearance racks at my favorite stores and buy cute items that I couldn't fit because "Somebody may need this super cute shirt, one day. I can't pass this up! It's only $3!"

Moment of truth here.

There was a period of time I truly enjoyed couponing and stockpiling. After doing it a few times, I saw how my family really benefited from it. But I also quickly realized how what I was doing was wrong. I ignored the gentle nudges of the Holy Spirit telling me to stop. The urges to get bundles, and clip coupons was insatiable. I continued to spend until my heart was content. We were headed for a collision.

I continued to break budgets set by my husband. In my mind, a budget was something that I should consider, but not necessarily adhere to. Consequently, I acted as if there was no budget.

I tried to soften the blow for my shopping sprees by making sure I had something for my husband. He would be okay until he saw the other 30 bags that were strewn across the backseat of the car.

Sales were my weakness. CVS, Walgreens, Meijers, and Kroger had weekly sales. I even knew their restocking dates. It was as if I felt compelled, almost guilty for missing a sale. One time, there was a sale on dishwashing liquid and a "q" (coupon) that made these beauties nearly free. Instead of spending $140 for 40 bottles, I could get them for only $30! My husband's question was always, "Baby, why do we need 40 bottles of dishwashing liquid?" My response? We could be stocked for the rest of the year! Never mind that we had 2 small children and could barely pay our rent. I had to feed my addiction.

If he said no, I would pull the money from somewhere else, create something and sell it or work the massage business to get the money I needed to catch those deals. I would burn gas going to 6 different stores just to find the same items before the other couponers cleared the shelves. I was out of control. I couldn't stop.

One day I looked up and our 3rd bedroom was filled with toilet paper, paper towels, shampoo and conditioner that we didn't need, dishwashing liquid, dozens of packs of pens, deodorant, toothpaste, wipes, and more. Sure, it may sound great, but at what expense?

I remember a time when the newspaper delivery guys didn't hit my block. They came every Tuesday at 11 am like clockwork. But this day, they didn't show up. I drove around my neighborhood looking for vacant houses so I could take their newspapers. I grabbed as many as I could with no shame.

One day, I asked my husband to come with me while I went to my coupon dealer's house. Yep, I had a connection. I had to go to the side door, pay her so much per bundle. Once the transaction was made, I happily walked out with at least 6 bundles of papers.

Everything came to a screeching halt when we were evicted. We had to pack up everything, place it in storage and stay in a hotel for 4 weeks. At this point, survival was everything. We eventually spent all of our savings between the hotels, fast food, storage fees, gas and repairs for both of our cars (which both broke down while we were living in hotels). There was nothing left to shop with. None of the excess toilet paper or shampoo could save us. I fell into depression. Not only because I couldn't shop, but because of the state of our marriage. Our negligence to follow the Holy Spirit, heed wise counsel, be responsible, and manage our finances wisely put us on the path to financial ruin.

Let's push pause. This story sounds more so like my addiction was due to my husband's personal issues. This is not true. There were deeper issues I hadn't discovered, yet. It took the Lord showing me... me. The little girl that felt insecure and uncovered by her parents. The teenager that craved to feel validated and told she was worth something more than giving herself away. The young adult that scrambled to understand what it meant to be loved, trust others, be a mature adult, how to manage money, etc. I wasn't taught these things earlier in life. As a result, I learned to be independent and do whatever I needed to do to take care of myself and make sure I felt happy and accepted in the process.

The shopping addiction was just a coverup to the deep-seated insecurities and trust issues that the Lord wanted to heal me from. My mind and heart needed a complete makeover. The whole process seemed scary, but once I decided to surrender my broken heart, unrealistic expectations, and insecurities to Him, I began to breathe again. My husband was absolutely supportive of my healing and growth, and still is.

Now, the process of our mindset changing regarding finances is another story. We continued moving in blissful (but extremely painful) ignorance until we decided to heed the wisdom given to us at our church regarding finances. Now, I'm not saying I leaped for joy over learning that I'm not a good financial steward. It took time to get there. But I was willing and wanted to change. Today, we are faithful tithers. Because of God's faithfulness to us, we have several savings accounts and other financially sound things in place. Things we never considered to be important before, we now have established. We love giving and sowing. God has continued to increase us. We are on the path to debt freedom. The only major bill is our mortgage and my student loan debt. We are still planning for our financial future.

We are in a totally different season in our life now. While I still do enjoy shopping, I know I cannot afford to spend frivolously - so I don't. Thank God, I exercise self-control! When my husband sets budgets, I do not break them. You may laugh at this, but I pray before I shop. Yes, before I go in stores, most times I ask the Lord to help me see sales and deals that I wouldn't normally see. Because of this, I often spend less than I intended. Everything that's posted as a deal really isn't a deal. We can ask the Lord to show us what to purchase and what not to purchase and He will.

In this chapter, we shared 2 of our specific addictions to help bring light to what we struggled with individually, how our choices and responses to stress (or triggers) affected our marriage, and how the Lord helped us to get out. You may not be able to relate to being addicted to shopping or games. However, there are countless others to consider. No matter what your struggle may be, we pray that you would come out of hiding and submit it to the Lord.

Here are a few things we have done and sometimes still practice to break addictions:

- **Above everything else, pray.**
    - Ask the Lord for help in every area where you are weak. Consult the Lord before making decisions and wait for Him to answer. Doing this can save

us from making unwise choices and enduring unnecessary pain. Psalm 18:6,

- **Seek & keep accountability**

    o You and your spouse must agree when selecting who your accountability will be. It would be wise to choose someone who is mature in the faith and not bias. That means, your best friend might not fit the description. James 5:16, Proverbs 11:14

- **Identify your triggers**

    o It's not enough to know what you are addicted to without first identifying what "takes you there". We suggest praying together and having a heart-to-heart talk with your spouse to help with this. Ask the Lord to reveal things that you cannot see. Do not abandon your spouse when he or she is triggered. Instead, work together to help them through it.

- **Examine your "whys"**

    o It's always a good thing to examine your motives vs. doing things out of comfort, haphazardly, or out of routine. Doing this will help you to identify unhealthy patterns. Devise a plan to help re-route your mind and behaviors when triggered. Psalm 119:59

- **Exercise your faith**
    - After identifying the addiction, it is imperative for you to immediately move on what the Word instructs us to do. Know that He is able to keep you from falling. Jude 24, James 2:17, Psalm 121:5,7

- **Communicate**
    - Sometimes women feel that their husbands should just "know". We don't want to tell him how we feel about anything. This kind of unrealistic expectation is unfair to the husband and harmful to the marriage.
    - Sometimes men feel like their wives "don't need to know" certain things. Because they pridefully feel they have everything under control. They may refuse to become vulnerable, as they may feel it is a sign of weakness. Spending time in prayer and with each other will help you to develop trust within your union where you feel safe to share anything without fear of backlash. It is important for each spouse to clearly communicate their feelings, desires, misunderstandings, and

requests. How else will they know? Proverbs 15:1, Proverbs 31:11

- **Examine the house and what's in it**

    o Earlier we spoke about how the addiction is the house, or coverup, for the deeper sin issues we were hiding. Be honest about where you are. We have to allow God to peel back the layers of hurt, shame, guilt, pain, and whatever else we are trying to avoid experiencing so that He can get to the root of the issue. Without identifying the real problem, the addiction is bound to come back. Maybe even in a different form. Two easy ways to identify an addiction is if you are choosing that thing over God or your spouse, and if you find yourself struggling to give something up, you could be addicted. 2 Corinthians 13:5

This short list of tips above can be applied to your life no matter what the stronghold may be.

We hope by reading our stories that you understand that an addiction is much more than the act itself. As stated before, the addiction is what houses the deeper sin issue that we are trying to hide. We pray that you would surrender whatever you are clinging to outside of Christ. Repent, and be healed so that you can be free and the Lord can get glory from your marriage.

Bio

Tony & Aries Winans have been married for more than 13 years And have 4 amazing children: Anthony, Aiden, Alonna, and Austin and their adorable dog, Alpha. Together they pastor Greater Works Family Ministries in Detroit and lead the marriage ministry, Club 1. They are both authors and have published a book together, entitled, "Life After I Do".

Contact info:

Pastors Tony & Aries Winans

Club 1 – Couples in Love United in the Body

Email: info@gwfmchurch.org

Website: gwfmchurch.org

TWO
After an Affair

By Pastors Carleton and Angela Booker

Special Forces Marriage Ministry

Many years ago, we experienced infidelity in our marriage. It was hell! But instead of destroying our family with a divorce, attorney costs, court appearances, and mandated family counseling, we took a step back and made a true commitment to God and to our marriage. Although it wasn't easy, we decided we wouldn't give up. We worked to revive the trust, forgiveness, and love between us and saw the purpose of our marriage without the truckload of infidelity issues.

Since then, we have helped hundreds of couples who have struggled with infidelity in their relationship. It can be difficult, but you can move past the pain, learn to forgive, and trust and love each once more. Next to losing a child, infidelity is often one of the most painful experiences couples go through.

Infidelity is pain created by betrayal, and thus, healing is necessary when you decide to continue the relationship.

Infidelity is a damaging event in a relationship, and it can be challenging to move beyond. It's also incredibly prevalent in our society, so we must talk about it. Unfortunately, the safer you feel with someone, the more painful infidelity will be when it occurs. It can be debilitating and feel like what we would call *emotional murder*.

Emotional murder is one of the worst emotional pains a person can experience. Dissecting infidelity hurts so badly is necessary for the healing process. Through this, we can understand why it's so difficult to forgive someone when they've hurt us so deeply.

Most people who experience infidelity have a lot of questions. This experience can bring about a lot of unknowns, especially for Christians. Marriage is a lifelong commitment, and yet, you or your partner violated an integral part of your covenant. Can your marriage survive at all? How can you move forward? What will God have waiting for you in the future? What direction does He want your life to take? How could God possibly have "let" this happen in the first place?

Don't lose hope. Your marriage can survive and come out of this stronger than ever. You can work through infidelity with God's guidance. You will also need patience, effort, and time. Here are our recommendations for how you can move forward as a couple.

End the affair. This is the first step you must take to rebuild trust in your relationship. You must end the affair entirely and understand how you want to handle the other person involved in the affair in daily life. Most people prefer to cut all contact with the individual. However, this isn't always possible. In some cases, the individual involved may be a close friend or family member. Thus, you and your spouse must agree on how you'll handle any interactions in the future.

Here are some questions that you should ask yourself during this period.

- Do I know for certain that the affair is over?

- Do I trust that an affair won't happen again in the future?

- Can I forgive my partner and the person they had an affair with?

- What do I expect from my spouse and the person they had an affair with?

As you work through this difficult event, you may need to alter certain elements of your current life like work, social situations, and family occasions. Take this in stride. So much change can feel uncomfortable for many, but if you can endure change, you can rebuild a marriage that was healthier than before.

Make healing your priority. If you want your marriage to survive, you must put healing first. This means making space for you and your spouse to heal before moving forward. Carve out time for reflection and invite God into this process. Pray to Him for strength and healing. It can be okay to separate for a time but put God at the center of this time. He can help draw you back together.

Establish a new normal. Consider incorporating daily prayer and affirmations with God into this routine. You can also seek religious counsel if you feel you need a third party to help you work through your thoughts. Additionally, you and your partner may find it helpful to read the Bible together. After you're spiritually fed, make sure you're getting enough exercise, continuing your own hobbies, and sleeping well. You can lean on God to help promote healing as you adjust to this new schedule.

Set and agree on boundaries. To salvage your marriage, you must set boundaries that help you rebuild trust. Discuss how you and your partner want to share space moving forward. It can feel difficult for many to return to shared space and intimacy. Addressing these issues head-on can help you cope with the discomfort you're feeling. Decide whether you're comfortable sharing a bedroom, having sex, holding hands, hugging, etc. It's okay if the answer is no to some or all these things right now but being on the same page with one another is essential. Overall, your goal should be to meet each other's physical and emotional needs.

Seek forgiveness. If you commit infidelity in your marriage, you must seek forgiveness from both your spouse and God. This is a process that involves many steps to acquire forgiveness from both. First, apologize to your spouse and recognize the pain that you've created for them. You cannot apologize in word alone; you must also apologize in action by committing to change and regaining their trust. Infidelity and adultery are not taken lightly in the Bible, but forgiveness is possible with God's love and grace. John [8:11] states, "'Then neither do I condemn you,'" Jesus declared. 'Go now and leave your life of sin.'"

Go to counseling. Going to a relationship counselor or a member of your church can help. Many people seek the help of a traditional counselor. However, your Christian community can also be a source of support and guidance during this time. Decide with your spouse the best path for support and advice at this time. Because infidelity can harm your relationship with God, religious counsel can help you get back on the right track. Find someone in your church to Bible study with; Bible passages highlighting the source of hope and strength can often be useful during this time.

Address the cause of the affair. Dealing with the cause of infidelity can help you heal and prevent other hurtful incidents. Dissatisfaction in a relationship is a common cause of infidelity. Understand why the disloyal partner had the affair. Was there something missing in the marriage? Were emotional and physical needs not being met? Seeking to understand the needs of your spouse should be a top priority. You should address the need for sexual intimacy, but feel free to return to it when you feel comfortable. Bear in mind that if you don't address the root cause of the affair then you cannot fix the relationship long-term. You'll simply be in the same relationship that led to infidelity.

See your spouse from God's perspective. Every one of us is made in His image. His grace and His love surpass all pain. It may feel difficult to see through your pain now; but consider the best parts of your partner — what God may love most. What would make it possible for God to forgive him or her? Because this might be challenging in the beginning, save this step for a time when you can see your spouse has put considerable effort into rebuilding your relationship. We suggest writing these qualities down to have something to refer to when you're struggling. It can also serve as a reminder of your progress.

Attend church regular services. A new, stronger relationship with God can help your marriage heal. Make an effort to attend regular church services together. This is quality time together that can prove helpful when you're learning to trust again. It can help you rebuild your relationship and lean on your religious community for support. If the other person involved in the affair also attends your current church, you may consider going to a different church until you're ready to encounter them (if you decide that's possible for you and your partner). Getting support from a new community can offer new perspectives and guidance as well as open your heart and soul to God.

Let yourself feel grief. To help your marriage survive, allow yourself to feel the grief that was thrust upon you. It may feel tempting to shove down your emotions — which are likely all negative — about the affair. However, it's nearly impossible to do this without a negative impact long-term. Allow yourself to feel your grief. Journal your thoughts and emotions, and when you feel ready, discuss those emotions with your partner.

Opening up is a good demonstration that trust is there. If you're a victim of infidelity or are the one who had an affair, you need to express your emotions clearly and safely. Addressing those feelings will help you both. It's important not to rush this part to move on to better things. Being open with your partner about what you're feeling can allow you to rebuild trust between you.

As painful as infidelity is, remember God wants what's best for you. In Jeremiah 29:11, it says "For I know the plans I have for you,' declares the Lord, 'plans to prosper you and not to harm you, plans to give you hope and a future.'" Passages like these can help inspire motivation and allow your marriage to endure through the toughest of times. Take the time to read these passages with your partner or share them when you find them during your independent Bible study.

Forgiveness and commitment are key for marriages to survive tough times. Your partner is unlikely to "get over it" or "change" without help. You must both be committed to work to improve your relationship. If you can display forgiveness and commitment in your relationship, there's hope you can come out victoriously on the other side.

It's essential that you disclose everything related to the affair, so you can identify what you must work through together. It is a process that you must go through for healing and forgiveness. If God can raise Jesus from the dead, can he not raise your dead marriage? If we truly trust him, we must trust him in all areas of our life.

Do you remember your wedding vows? You stood in front of each other and God and declared, "For better or for worse." This could be your "worse." Marriage comes with the good, the bad. and the ugly. Just remember this when Satan comes talking to you about your marriage. In Romans 8:2, it says, "And we know that for those who love God all things work together for good, for those who are called according to his purpose."

Your marriage has a purpose beyond you and your partner! You two are a living testimony of God on Earth. You are two imperfect people joined together for life. God is the one in the middle of your marriage that makes your marriage perfect. God is the super glue in the marriage. Without him, it all falls apart. The power of prayer in your marriage is so important.

The Bible talks about the power of two in Matt 18:19 which says, "Again, I tell you that if two of you on earth agree about anything you ask for, it will be done for you by my Father in Heaven. For where two or three come together in my name, there am I with them."

If you want your marriage free of infidelity, ask the Lord, and it will be done in Jesus' name. Make your marriage a kingdom marriage. There is life in the power of the tongue. Proverbs 18:21 says, Death and life *are* in the power of the tongue: and they that love it shall eat the fruit there KJ, what are you speaking? life or death? speak life; you have the power.

Bio

Special Forces Marriage Ministry is a Ministry that is passionate about divorce-proofing marriages within the church, our communities and the state. Founded by Carleton & Angela Booker, married over 44 years. They have a wealth of wisdom and kingdom knowledge to restore marriages back to God's original intention. With more than 25 years of ministry experience together, they are dedicated to free marriages from the grip of the enemy (Satan) and to help married couples avoid the enemy's mission of divorce and destruction. Our marriage ministry motto is DE OPPRESSO LIBE, it is the same Special Forces term in the military. It is translated from Latin to mean, "To liberate the oppressed". The oppressed refers to the state of all married couples in America. However, we strongly believe who the Son sets free is free indeed (John 8:36 KJV).

Contact info:

Email: info@marriedcouplescoachingcouples.com

Website: marriedcouplescoachingcouples.com

THREE

For Richer or Poorer: Drowning in Debt

Oscar & Crystal Jones

Marriage for a Lifetime Ministries

We started out in our marriage accumulating debt and found ourselves drowning under its weight, years later. We bought whatever we *felt* we needed at the time...on credit. And nearly everything was considered a need. There was no method to our madness. We had no budget. No wisdom. No counsel. And zero savings for many years. We were both haphazard in our approach to money.

I (Crystal) liked having a lot of credit cards. It made me feel empowered. I felt like the credit cards made up for our financial lack. I believed that the credit limit extended our income. I had credit cards to stores for plus-sized women. I couldn't shop for myself in these stores. In those days, I wore a size 2 to size 4. However I got the card to shop for the plus-sized members of my extended family. I even had a credit card to Saks Fifth Avenue. The plastic genie granted us access to places we should have never been.

We had a lot of debt and a lot of headaches because of it. As a result it put extra stress on our marriage.

If you find yourself here, we hope to encourage you. While you may have so much debt that you can't see a way out, don't lose hope. Today, we are debt-free except for our mortgage, which we have on an acceleration plan for cancelation. (In 2 ½ years, we have cancelled roughly $20,000). We have a spending and savings plan. We have multiple savings accounts. And we will leave a sizable inheritance to our children and grandchildren.

The crazy thing about all of this is *we didn't* receive some huge windfall or inheritance. No one stepped in to rescue us. We didn't file bankruptcy.

As crazy as it is, we actually became debt-free *after* my husband lost his job and we had no income. Yes, you read that correctly. We became debt-free when we had no steady income. God gave us His plan and it worked. And if you are ready, it will work for you, too.

Let's begin by saying, "Money doesn't break up marriages". It's how we handle and think about money that causes all the trouble. We have to change the way we think in order to change our financial position. We have to learn how to depend on God together. It's as simple and complex as that.

Most often, people think that the problem is that they don't have enough money coming in. It really is not about *how much* we have. Because our approach will be the same regardless to the amount of cash we have. But it is really about our relationship with money and our relationship with our God. It's the mindset of our culture that keeps us locked in poverty's clenches. 'Chasing the bag' and 'Keeping up with the Joneses' will cost you. God meant for money to be a tool to help us, not something we worship or chase after. Money and material possessions are to never be our priority as believers. God is who we ought to seek first. His kingdom and His righteousness. Our finances won't change until the way we think about money does.

Our (Oscar & Crystal) relationship with God was the same as our money – hit or miss. We were up and down in our seek, half-hearted at best. We would seek God about things fervently when we had a pressing issue. Otherwise, we spent our money as we saw fit. We leaned to our own understanding. As a result, we argued about money and bills, most of the time.

Paying bills on time was not even on my (Oscar) agenda. From my viewpoint, the due date was a gentle nudge to start thinking about paying it. I didn't see it as a deadline. I also had to see what other bills I had before I decided *if* I was going to send the minimum payment requested.

On the other hand, I (Crystal) hated paying bills late and would often throw my husband under the proverbial bus when the bill collectors called. I wanted to protect my name. My credit score had become more important than protecting my husband. I wore my credit score as a badge of honor. Pride had allowed it to become an idol. We were both out of order. So as God does with idols, He allowed it to come crashing down. My credit score flopped to basement level right alongside my husband's.

We were both working and making decent money but still could not manage to make ends meet. We accused each other. But remained in the vicious cycle of poverty.

There was absolutely no planning for the future. The wisdom of God felt beyond us. We really believed, like most people, that we couldn't afford to save because we had too many bills and too little money. The sad thing is we never stopped to ask why.

We saw stewardship as something for those with *enough* money to do it. So we put it off for later. We didn't feel like we were 'on that level'. The truth is we just didn't know how to do any better and we weren't willing to seek out the solution. Looking back, it could have been because we were so embarrassed about where we were financially. We didn't understand most people were in the same position.

The only real way out of this mess was to confront the issue head on. God said if we are faithful over the little, He would make us ruler over much. When my husband and I aligned with what God was saying... I mean, really got into agreement, that's when we saw breakthrough.

We would progress 3 steps, but then would have a setback. We did have savings but still a lot of debt. I (Crystal) yearned for debt freedom. I (Oscar) didn't see debt freedom as attainable. After much persuasion, I (Crystal) finally got my husband to agree to do a debt consolation loan so we could have just one bill. It felt great. A year later, I discovered hubby had a secret credit card, this set us back again. The financial infidelity shook our marriage. I felt betrayed. Arguments ensued. We had to decide that we weren't going to let this break us. After much prayer and forgiveness, we finally came into agreement about keeping light (God) in our finances, avoiding secrets and lies.

Fast forward, years later, things got better again. The deeper in Christ, the better things became. Our minds had totally shifted. Saving was essential, regardless to the bills that were looming. We knew that we couldn't afford **not** to save. That was transformative thinking for us.

The Lord asked us to relocate to California for ministry. At the time, we had some debt and about $14,000 in savings. We took the leap of faith.

But after one year of living in the exorbitant state of California, I (Oscar) lost my job. We set stunned in disbelief with no income. It was a set-up. We were being pushed deeper into our trust and dependency on God.

God told us not to live off the unemployment checks, but to save them. He told us He would take care of us. We applied to other jobs. No one would hire either of us. It was crazy. I would often tell people when it doesn't make sense, "Look up, God may be involved." And sure enough that is what was happening. We were being launched into full-time ministry.

God began to speak often, clearly mapping out the plan that would get us to debt freedom. We downsized from a 3-bedroom house to a 2-bedroom apartment. This cut our lease payment in half. We asked God for His plan. And during this season with no jobs, we were not late one day paying our bills. God always provided. We saw so many miracles. Our utility bills showed a credit for over a year. Hospital bills came reading a zero balance.

God asked us what was in our hands. We wrote out all of your gifts, talents, and abilities. We wrote out all the licenses we possessed. And we prayed over the list. As we felt released, we began to use the gifts that God had given us to bring in finances. We started writing books. We also launched the Couples' Café in California. And doors swung open. We were doing Café's all over the Bay area. The more we followed God's plan, the more we prospered.

Don't misunderstand, this was no overnight testimony. We were in a season of deep sacrifice. It took us years of living by faith. We trusted God for every minor provision. We used what was in our hands to bring in income. The finances started coming in. God taught us how to be good stewards. We continued to save. Today, we are in a strong financial place because of God's guidance.

If your marriage is bleeding debt, stop, pray and get in agreement with the Lord. His plan is best. Cease all unnecessary spending for a season to course correct! Cut back on the extras. Cancel unnecessary subscriptions. Agree to only spend when you are both in agreement and you've prayed about it. This takes self-discipline.

When we buy what we want, when we want, we are *not* allowing God to be Lord over our finances. God absolutely must be first. He must be our Guide and #1 Financial Adviser.

Here are the lessons we learned along the way,

1. Repentance – the way we were handling money wasn't just irresponsible, it was sin. We identified greed, selfishness, and idolatry in our lives. You have to be able to identify the spirits that cause you to get in debt. After you repent, you must get God's heart on money. And live in it. So asking Him to renew your minds is paramount.

2. Pay your tithes and offerings regularly. This is an act of trust - putting Him first in your finances. Allow Him to manage 100% of what comes into your household. If you don't feel you are disciplined enough, set up on automatic payroll deduction.

3. Pray over your debt. Ask God for a debt cancellation plan. We learned to abhor debt. The Word tells us that the borrower is slave to the lender. We decided we didn't want to be slaves any longer. That meant that we would have to embrace the idea of *delayed gratification*. You don't have to have everything you want or even *need* right at the moment. God knows what you need and want. Trust Him to provide for you. If you can't afford it, that does not mean that you are supposed to become a slave to get it (by putting it on a credit card). Agree to make debt your enemy.

4. *Don't try to keep up with the Joneses.* Our culture will tell you that you deserve the greatest, the latest, the biggest, and the best. And if you don't have it, you are losing out and behind your peers. The truth is you aren't. In fact, you will be ahead because you won't have the debt of your peers. Don't upgrade something, simply because there is a newer model available. You should replace things that are damaged, broken, or obsolete. Avoid the temptation to accumulate more debt. We have to learn contentment. Often, we think we deserve something we

can't afford. It really is the influence of the culture. The culture tells you that you work hard, so indulge yourself. The message doesn't take in consideration, that you are the one guilty of accumulating the debt that you already have.

It is unjust to lavish yourself with pleasures and dodge paying those you owe. We are enslaved because we put ourselves and our pleasures above God. If we truly submit to Him. We would ask Him before making purchases. We would have less buyer's remorse if we would hearken to God's voice.

5. Put your money together in one pot as a couple. You will get to financial wealth faster if you are on one accord in your finances. Combine your incomes to attack the combined debt. There is power in agreement. You will waste more if you are managing your finances separately.

6. Set up 2 savings accounts (long term and short term) immediately. Set aside 10% of your household income to be split over all your savings accounts. Remember poverty says, "I can't afford to save." Wealth says, "I can't afford **not** to save." Choose to take on a wealthy mindset. Saving must be a priority.

The purpose of the long-term account is in the event either of you lose your job. You should have at least 8 months living expenses saved to carry you through.

The short-term account is your emergency account. This account is for unexpected expenses. If you have a flat tire or an appliance breaks down, you won't have to take it out of your household expense account. Build this account to $1,000 to $2,000. Agree on the amount that goes into each account every week or bi-weekly. These will not be your only savings accounts. This is just where you begin. Use payroll deduction to fund these accounts if you don't have the discipline.

Currently, my wife and I have many savings accounts and investments. We started with the 2 accounts and added on accounts as our finances were more secure.

7. Find out your debt-free number. Add up all of your liabilities: car payment, mortgage, credit cards, student loans, furniture cards, etc. These are not bills like electricity or water bill (except if there is a past balance). If someone ever approached you to write a check for all the debt you owe you should be able to give them that number. The Bible says know the state of your flocks. Proverbs 27:23

8. Create a spending plan that will work for your family and stick to it. The goal is to live *below* your income. Cut

expenses and add income. Use gifts and talents to bring in more wealth.

9. Give, give, give. As bad off as you believe you are, someone else is worse off. Sow. Allow the Lord to direct your giving. My husband and I keep seed in the ground. We give lavishly and God gives back to us in the same way that we give.

10. Sell things that you are not using that you could put towards your debt. There are so many cites that you can sell on, even social media.

11. Snowball your debt: Pay off your smallest debt first and as quickly as you can. Once that debt is paid, you take the money you were putting toward that payment and add it onto the next-smallest debt payment and so on. Continue until all accounts are paid off.

Buckle in. Debt-freedom won't happen instantly. It takes steady plodding or consistency. Don't give up. Read what the Bible has to say about finances. Learn as much as you can about financial stewardship and put it in practice. No longer see stewardship as a burden but a blessing and liaison to wealthy living. You will have much more wealth to pour into the kingdom of God.

Bio

Oscar & Crystal Jones have been celebrating their covenant love affair for more than 41 years. They have 8 children (which include 1 daughter-in-law and 2 sons-in-law). They are the happy grandparents of 11 delightful grandchildren.

Pastors Oscar & Crystal have a unique Aquila and Priscilla team ministry. They lavishly love the Lord and one another. God has coupled this into a special anointing and gifted them to be able to minister from the pulpit as one voice. Many marriages have been strengthened and healed. They have also witnessed marriages reconciled *even after divorce*.

The Joneses are leaders and founders of Marriage for a Lifetime Ministries, a 501c3 nonprofit organization. They host a monthly *Marriage Chat* on Facebook Live, The *Gathering of the Wives* held quarterly on Zoom where they discuss issues. They host *Couple's Cafes*, marriage conferences and retreats at churches across the U.S. They also sponsor a marriage retreat for senior pastors and their spouses only called, *Tending the Bride*. They pour their heart into helping marriages thrive.

These long-time honeymooners continue to have a heart for repairing the breaches in marriages and families.

They have been featured guests on several radio and television broadcasts.

The couple has authored more than 21 books total (together and apart). They aspire to leave a legacy of hope and healing to marriages and families all over the world.

Contact: Marriage for a Lifetime Ministries

Website:marriage4alifetime.org

Email: jones@marriage4alifetime.org

Fb: facebook.com/groups/marriage4alifetime.org

FOUR
Forsaking All Others: Priority of Marriage

Oscar & Crystal Jones

Marriage for a Lifetime Ministries

Remember the first time you knew you were in love with your spouse? You were head over heels wildly in love. It may have seemed he/she was the only one in a crowded room. When there was time to spend, you wanted to spend it with each other. The more time you spent the more you wanted to spend. You eventually said, "I do". After a while, life started to get in the way. Jobs, school, kids' activities, chores, errands, and other commitments caused you to lose focus and forget to prioritize the relationship that matters most.

Other than your relationship to God, your spouse should be the most important person in your life. We must be rooted in Jesus first if we're to love our spouses the way that God intended. The priority of God keeps our own lives in order.

"And he said to him, "You shall love the Lord your God with all your heart and with all your soul and with all your mind. This is the great and *first* commandment." (Matthew 22:37-38)

First denotes beginning, as in before anything or anyone else. God uses the word "first" in many passages of scripture to establish order for His people.

"But seek *first* the kingdom of God and his righteousness, and all these things will be added to you." (Matthew 6:33)

God's position is always primary. Before anything was, God was, will be, and still is. And He remains in that position even after marriage. However as a married couple, God requires us to position our spouses first, right after Himself. Putting and keeping your spouse in first place position is essential for a healthy marriage.

A spouse may not even recognize when he/she is putting their spouse in second or third place. It happens.

For example, a friend/family member may need help with something, and the spouse also needs help with something. Too often, the response is to expect the spouse to understand while you rush to aid of the other friend or family member. This is inconsiderate behavior.

Those spouses who are always ready and willing to help fix everyone else's problem but only offering aid to their spouse when it's convenient, signal to the spouse that they aren't in first position. Your husband or wife should be the first person you support, not the last.

When we talk about placing spouses in the first position above all other relationships, many people cringe. Some people think that children should be first. They don't quite understand. Setting your husband/wife as your priority doesn't mean neglecting, mistreating, or abusing your children.

On the contrary, God expects both parents to love, provide, nurture, and care for the children. God deals harshly with those who harm children. So this idea of prioritizing the spouse is not about overlooking the children. The spouse priority means that the children benefit from the love and leadership that pour from the couple who created that family unit. The two spouses are responsible to keep each other lifted up in a way that keeps the family unit intact. It is foundational to the healthy life of the family.

The husband and wife, as leaders of the family, make decisions out of love and respect. It is this leadership that must be held firmly in place to keep the rest of the family intact. And if they do it properly, the children will grow up, follow their example, and leave the nest to find their own spouses to prioritize. So we are never to place our children above our spouses.

Still some people think that their siblings should come before their spouses. Usually this idea comes in when there have been many divorces or never marrieds in the extended family. Regardless to the trauma, this is *not* the will of God. Siblings have their place, but never at the expense of the spouse. A sibling cannot be equal to or above a spouse. God does not intend for a bride to be one with her sister. Or a groom to be one with his brother. Your oneness is due to your spouse.

The same is true regarding parents. It is unnatural to have a mother and her son lead a marriage. Neither is it proper for one spouse to prioritize a parent over his/her one flesh partner. It is out of order and out of the will of God. The parents and parents-in-law do not take precedence in the marriage. God directed men to *leave his father and mother* to become one with his wife.

Genesis 2:24

Therefore shall a man leave his father and his mother, and shall cleave unto his wife: and they shall be one flesh.

Matthew 19:5 reiterates it, 'For this reason a man shall leave his father and mother and be joined to his wife, and the two shall become one flesh'?

The parental relationship is the most important relationship *before* a person marries. **But when a couple weds, God says that the spouse takes first position above all others except Himself.**

Still there are some who think that the church should come before the spouse. The church is the bride of Christ. It is misguided thinking to believe that Christ's bride is also the pastor's bride. A man is to have his own bride, and it is <u>not</u> the church. God won't share that position with another man. And He asks no one to sacrifice their family on the altar of ministry. The work we are called to is never before our own families. Jesus keeps His bride first and church leaders should keep their spouse first, following the example of Christ.

Let us be clear. No family, friend, child, job, or church should come before your spouse.

To create a successful and healthy covenantal union, we are asked to forsake ***all*** others and cleave to our spouses. All others include the exes, hobbies, coworkers, and other extended family members.

If we embrace the whole scriptures, it becomes clear the priority we are to give our spouses, in light of who Jesus is.

Wives, submit to your own husbands, as to the Lord. For the husband is the head of the wife even as Christ is the head of the church, his body, and is himself its Savior. Now as the church submits to Christ, so also wives should submit in everything to their husbands. Husbands, love your wives, as Christ loved the church and gave himself up for her...

Christ's first priority after loving and obeying the Father is his bride, the Church. *In the same way,* our next love, after God, should be our spouses. Christ gave his life for his bride out of obedience to God. He loved us even to the point of death! How much more are we to give our love to our spouses?

What does it mean to put your spouse first?

- First place starts with God. As we seek to please Him our actions and thoughts will reflect His priority. If we acknowledge him in all your ways, He will direct our path. Ask Him for His guidance. He can teach us how to properly love and cherish our spouses.

- Listen to your spouse. Be attentive and responsive. Give them your full attention when they are speaking. Put down the cell phone, cut off the television and video games. Value his/her input.

- Make sure you spend enough time together. Healthy couples "make" time for one another. They don't just hope that it will happen or try to find the time. It is important enough to schedule. So intentionally schedule weekly date nights. Also plan husband-wife meetings (to deal with the issues that come up).

- It is important that we make sure our spouse feel secure and esteemed in the relationship. That means consulting him/her before making plans or decisions. It is not fair to assume that our spouse is okay or won't mind if you take an action. It is respectful to ask them how they feel about something and how it will impact them. Talk it out to find the best solutions that work for you both.

If you take on a second job, go back to school, or a secure a different position with more responsibilities, it will affect your whole family. Talk about what items will be left undone as a result. Talk about the extra stress and new expenses that will incur, and the time taken away from the family. Work together to mitigate as much overload and stress as possible. Prepare to add in extra support, a housekeeping service, childcare or lawn service. And carve in time to purposely connect with the family.

- Understand that couples do not have to do everything together, all of the time. It is healthy to do things separately, occasionally. Enjoy family and friends separately sometimes. It makes coming together that much more satisfying.

- Demonstrate loyalty when there is a conflict with others. Do not side with your family or friends or make jokes at your spouse's expense. At some point, it may become necessary to confront your own parents/siblings about their words or actions toward your spouse. Parents sometime struggle with their adjusted role when you marry. You have to help them adapt by speaking up and drawing clear boundaries.

When a spouse doesn't speak up in defense of his/her spouse when she/he is under attack it is undermining that first priority position. Silence often equals agreement. So if your spouse is being attacked by your family or friends, speak up. Even if your spouse is wrong, use wisdom to handle the situation so that he/she does not feel attacked. Whatever you do, do something. Don't stand there and watch it happen. Your spouse needs to feel that you will choose them over everyone else.

Keeping your spouse in first place is no easy task. Life goes through various seasons. And there will be the need to check in with each other and adjust to make sure each spouse keeps the other in that first-place position. Remember you only have a limited time to be married on this earth. Use your time wisely. Follow God's law of first place and you'll enjoy a healthy, successful marriage.

FIVE
Grief: Ain't Nobody got Time for that!

Ralph & LaShawnda Williams

FAMM (Forsaking all others Marriage Ministry)

Tears streamed down my face as I (LaShawnda) sat in the car in my driveaway and stared out into space for a span of an hour or more. It finally occurred to me **"I am not okay."** As strong as I had seemed to have been, at this point, I was completely broken. A few years had passed since the death of my uncle, my surrogate father...the man who gave me away at my wedding. Sudden illness led to hospice care at my home until his death. Two weeks later, I was back at work and life went back to normal with regularly scheduled activities. Six months after, my grandfather died. Years later, as I sat in my driveway, it had all finally caught up with me.

What's unique about grief? Probably the fact that it is not unique at all. Of all the hardships we experience in our marriages, grief is pretty much guaranteed to be universal. As a matter of fact, we would not expect many objections if we converted the standard wedding vows:

"For better, for worse, for richer, for poorer, in sickness and health, _through grief, trauma and loss,_ to love and to cherish, until death do us part."

Grief occurs as a response to the death of loved ones, in light of traumatic events, and/or after losing valuable relationships or positions in life (think of an injured police officer or person experiencing dementia). We, as couples, experience these moments both individually and collectively, very often with no warning or preparation. Grief is the notorious party crasher, the unwanted house guest, the gift that you wish you could send back!

Contrary to popular belief there is no standard means of quantifying grief. One family's loss of a pet can be just as devastating as another's loss of an aunt or uncle. The experiences are different, but the impact can be the same. A loss is just that, whether a parent, co-worker, job, or family pet, the extent of the grief goes as deep as the love that they had for those individuals.

As we are currently amid a pandemic, with over 1,000,000 lives lost and countless others forever changed, our collective pain is palpable. Over the past few years, we (Team Williams) have personally experienced the loss of many family members, some of old age, some from illness, and some from unspeakable tragedies. We have also suffered the breakdown of some of our closest relationships. In addition, Ralph, being a physician, has experienced an overwhelming amount of loss with both patients and colleagues. We're actively grieving. We are well aware that we are not the only ones. We invite you to engage in this journey with us as we commit to being better partners looking to the source of all comfort!

Stages of Grief

For the sake of this chapter, we will address grief in the 5 stages as originally presented in medical science and coined by Elisabeth Kubler-Ross (On Death and Dying). Of course, there is no perfect model to define something so personal. Although presented in stages, grief is very adept at overriding our guidelines. Instead of looking at things step-by-step, we can better be served by understanding it as 'grief stew' or 'grief casserole'. You know, all the ingredients mixed in together. Nevertheless, each of these aspects of grief play an important role in our marriages and home life.

Denial takes place, usually at the onset of a loss or traumatic experience. You have a tendency to be "numb" or zoned out, which may be necessary to accomplish tasks associated with a loss as well as everyday life. Sometimes, you will unintentionally cause more harm to self by not acknowledging the impact that a certain event has had on your life. Men in particular, have a difficult time with this. Our society places demands on us that cannot wait until we get ourselves together. Hence, we carry an illusion of strength when we are really hurting inside. We are unable to meet expectations of ourselves or others and set ourselves up for failure.

I (Ralph) remember when we lost one of our church members to suicide. I'm tearing up as I write. For months, I carried on as though I was not allowed to, nor had the time to mourn as we navigated work, church, kids, etc. However, one Sunday morning, I actually got lost while driving to church, a trip I have taken hundreds of times. Denial and suppression will discombobulate even the simplest of things. What I needed ... a good cry. I eventually got it, how about you?

Anger presents as overall moodiness, being easily offended, sometimes a desire for "revenge" or finding someone or something to blame. Although a natural part of the process, anger causes distance with your spouse, leaking of emotions, irritability, and bitterness. The Bible says be angry and sin not. Our prayer is that during these times, we allow these emotions to run their course without taking over our lives. In these moments, we ask for God to overwhelm us with His love so our compassion and love won't be shut off. We again affirm that this is all a part of the process. Hence, give yourself a break. You might need to vent to your partner or cry out to God. Always leave room for the peace of God above all things.

In times of grief, we may want to **bargain with God**. We can find ourselves confused and questioning God's will. Our prayers can go from a means of comfort and instruction to a means to manipulate or attempt to change God's mind. We are given free access to cast our cares on Him; but must accept that we cannot '*cast our will upon Him*'. Sometimes, you won't feel like praying. Thank God that he continues to intercede for us (Ro. 8:26-27).

Depression can present itself in many ways. There are the obvious; crying spells, insomnia, lack of motivation to get up in the morning, and substance use. These are overt signs of clinical depression. There are also the more subtle indicators; moodiness, over-sleeping/overeating, failure to fully complete tasks. In your home life, depression has a way of stifling your emotional and physical availability. It can create barriers in your marriage and really change the atmosphere of your home. Let's be clear, everyone experiences some form of depression at times. Ignoring our reality can delay our healing.

Acceptance, unfortunately, is not the phase where you are pain free. We look forward to that day in heaven. Rather, this becomes the moment that you find true peace with God's will and have committed to walking out your new normal. Your prayer life is balanced and although your home life may still be recovering, you have started the healing process. As mentioned, grief doesn't follow rules, so you should expect the occasional "Kablam!" The key is to look to God along this journey, hear his voice, get wise counsel, and never abandon your spouse.

For the Grieving

It is okay to feel. Grief, loss, and trauma throw a monkey wrench into your well-oiled machine. Our society and (more often than we're comfortable admitting) our churches are fast paced with high demands and an expectation for us to just "get over it." However, Jesus himself demonstrated emotions and is fully acquainted with ours (Heb. 4:15; John 11:35). **If God, who is our standard, has feelings, why wouldn't you and I?** It is important that you acknowledge your emotions fully and allow time to deal with them. Contrary to what some may say, vulnerability, pain, and weakness are not in opposition to faith. In truth, these moments allow for God to become more evident in your life. His healing for our broken hearts. His comfort for our mourning (Is. 61:1-2). His strength in our weakness (2 Cor. 12:19).

You are not crazy! Deal with your emotions. Own them! Give it time and allow God to heal them. Also, therapy isn't a bad word. There are times where you will need extra support from someone trained to help you navigate your emotions. I

(LaShawnda) sought help from a Christian counselor who proved instrumental to my process.

It is okay to fail. God didn't call us to be perfect, so please take the pressure off yourself. In these seasons, God calls us to rest and find strength in Him. We cannot be too busy to deal with ourselves. God cares more about our well-being than deadlines, promotions, projects, church services, events, and perfect meals. You will let people down. Even in our marriages, we will find that we can't always meet expectations. God understands; and your spouse will learn to, as well. When we truly let go of being in control, God has a way of continuing to keep the universe going, even without our help!

In marriage, communication is key. Let's be honest, it's hard to communicate what you do not know or fully understand. Sometimes we don't even have the words to describe what we are feeling. As much as we are aware, we should not leave our spouses in the dark when we grieve. Talk to them about the pain of your loss. Do not hide, suppress or deny your feelings. Also, agree with them on expectations during these times. If you can't speak, write a letter. Satan would love to fill in the gaps and tell his version of the story to your spouse when you are silent. Sometimes your spouse will understand, other times, they won't. Please don't be offended. This is an opportunity to grow together. Pray often allowing God to fill your cup and strengthen your unity.

Unfortunately, **there are no shortcuts** through the grieving process. Grief has no deadline. Often, our attempts to "keep it moving" actually prolong the process. Even those who may feel like their grief is over will experience a rude awakening! This is something that we must go through.

For the Spouse: This is your Assignment

Generally speaking, when others experience loss, we may pray for them, provide a meal, and even help with some of the arrangements. However, walking alongside someone the following weeks, months and years is a totally different story. As a husband/wife, these are the cherished opportunities for you to "rise to the occasion". You become the protector, tear wiper, meal preparer, and sounding board. What we begin to understand is that grief and loss <u>change us</u>. We have the privilege of loving and serving our partners as they go through this process. You will deal with mixed messages, emotional rollercoasters, confusing speech and an inability to meet the previously established expectations. Find joy in the fact that God has equipped you to be everything that you need to be during this season.

Be Patient. During this season, lavish your spouse with grace. This applies even when you think that they don't deserve it. Your kindness goes far with your spouse, and it can serve to help heal their wounds. Your words carry so much power during this time. Do not wield insults or speak to them harshly. **Do not tell them to "get over it."**

As a spouse, do not compare grief. Each person is different because they are uniquely made by God. It would not be fair for you to compare your grief to theirs and how you would handle things if you were them. This is not a competition. We do not get to determine what is considered traumatic and what is not for someone else.

Know that your grieving spouse is just as confused as you are. To be embraced and met with love in the midst of the internal chaos is soothing. Knowing that you have someone that will walk with you through these trying times with no expectations of perfection serves as comfort to the grieving soul.

This is also a time to agree on lowered expectations of your spouse. Maybe they can't perform around the house, on their job, or even in the bedroom, as before. Maybe laundry piles up, oil changes get missed or the kid's homework slips a little. Give grace. It is during these times that we learn what is most important.

Be prayerful. Pray without ceasing (1 Th 5:17). Pray not only for your spouse to be healed, but also to make your heart more sensitive to your spouse's needs. Be mindful that it may not always be a good idea to start "laying hands" and "praying the heavens down" when they are showing signs of grief. You must also be careful not to use prayer to push your will onto your

<u>spouse</u>. Your care, compassion and intentionality should preach the Gospel to them. Prayer will give you foresight to things that you can do to support your partner. It will increase your patience and expand your capacity during the most trying times.

Be Present. As a lifelong partner, your spouse should be worth your time and attention. It may prove wise to work less hours, unless mandatory (ex: first responder or military). It would also be prudent to spend less time doing extracurricular activities. As much as you may feel these things are important, <u>nothing</u> is more important than your assignment to your spouse. Make sure that your spouse knows that they are your number one priority.

I (Ralph) recall one time, I was planning an event for my church while my wife was actively experiencing a grief trigger. I was so focused on getting to the church that I neglected to be present for my wife. My solution: "Why don't you come up and join the choir rehearsal? That should cheer you up!" Needless to say, that backfired! The reality is that I was so focused on my plans, that I failed to *see* my wife. Consequently, she stayed at home alone, feeling unvalued and unloved!

You must be present both physically and mentally. Pay attention to holidays, anniversaries, and certain triggers. Because grief is so unpredictable, we can go from crying to smiling to frowning to laughing to yelling in thirty seconds or less. The easiest solution seems to just leave this person alone;

they are "all over the place". We have found that the opposite is often true, especially with women. Don't leave them, even when things are awkward. If they request alone time, grant it. However, make sure that you stay close and be ready to reconnect.

Be Practical. Find practical ways to bring them joy. Consider their love language and make extra effort to "fill their love tank" (5 love languages, Chapman). If they enjoy gifts, make sure you bring something home to let them know that you were thinking of them. If they enjoy acts of service, go out of your way to help around the house. If they enjoy physical touch, give them a massage. Plan times for them to get away. This can be a weekend trip or dedicated leisure time. Lower overall expectations and look for ways to alleviate your spouse's burden. Plan to compensate for three to six months during periods of acute grief. From then on, let prayer and communication guide you.

Let's talk about sex. Sex is a gift from God that strengthens our bond and gives us pleasure. During times of grief, sex can either be an overbearing demand or an appreciated act of love for the bereaved. Know your spouse and prayerfully consider the role of sex during this time. Submit yourself to the Lord for strength if a period of restraint is necessary (1Cor 7:5).

When We Both Are Hurting

What happens when both of you feel "like you don't have it to give"? How do you navigate the pain of losing a child or a major traumatic event that leaves you both in desperate need of comfort? As a couple, you'll experience most losses and life transitions together. God promises that two are better than one...even more a three-fold cord is not easily broken (Ecc. 4:9-10). In these seasons, the key is to hold on to each other and allow God to heal you both.

Satan would love to use every opportunity to put a wedge between you and your spouse. What better way than to take advantage of your sensitive feelings, anger, or depression. You must be careful to keep communication open and commit to doing things that draw you close. Embrace each other, touch each other, serve each other. An older couple once shared with us, that soon after receiving news about the death of their son they embraced one another and made love. This act confirmed their covenant and union during the most painful time.

Note that you and your spouse will grieve differently. There is no right way or wrong way. Each of you must go through your own processes. Don't be tempted to compare or compete. If tense moments arise, remember that you are partners, grab hands and push through the awkwardness. Trust God to be everything that you need, and you will grow stronger together.

A Word on CHILDREN

Children in the home experience the same ups and downs that we do. In areas of grief and loss, they can be impacted the same and sometimes more than the parents. It was not just your mom who passed, it was their grandma. It wasn't just your friendship that dissolved, it was their support system.

Each child is different, so they may express pain or loss in different ways. Some may seem to be okay on the exterior but are crying inside. If we, as adults, don't know how to feel about these instances, just imagine how lost our children may be. As they navigate these losses with you, it may be prudent to consider practical ways to bring your children joy during these difficult times. Send them on vacation, take them to their favorite place, cover their chores or even get them a gift just because. Think of things that can be done to lighten their load and minister to them.

Due to your own grief, you won't always get things right. Never be too proud to apologize to your children when you have mishandled them. Seek avenues of support for them and work on total healing as a family.

Happy Endings

For everything there is a season and a time for every purpose under heaven: a time to be born, and a time to die...a time to heal...a time to weep, and a time to laugh; a time to mourn (Ec.

3:1-8). This passage lets us know that grief is a part of life that should be expected. We encourage you to take this opportunity to pause and heal so that you can be healthy. That day will come when there will be no more tears (Rev 21:4). Until then, we have promises that God will never leave us (Ps. 139:7). In the end, this process will strengthen you both as individuals and as a couple. Know that you are loved, you are valuable and you're worth the effort it takes to be whole again.

We dedicate this chapter to the memory of Kenneth James Sr., one of the many lost during the COVID-19 pandemic. Thank you for introducing us to Marriage for a Lifetime Ministries

Bio

Ralph and LaShawnda Williams are native Detroiters who originally met in high school. Married in 2004, they have been active in multiple areas of ministry since 2003 and active in marriage ministry since 2015. Founders of "Forsaking all others Marriage Ministry" (The FAMM),

Ralph and LaShawnda brings an old-school flavor to the new millennial marriage emphasizing both the spiritual and practical elements that contribute to a "championship marriage". Their home life is never dull as they balance ministry, careers and raising their three teen/preteen children.

Contact: FAMM (Forsaking All Others Marriage Ministry

Email: thefammlife@gmail.com

SIX

In Sickness and in Health

Mark & Sherri Bryant

Lifeline Marriage Ministry

Our marriage has been a 38-year adventure, experienced through the years like changing seasons.

'Mark and Sherri against the world', was the way our young minds looked at love. In early September 1984, at the tender ages of 22 and 26, our marriage vows were taken before the Lord and in the presence of many witnesses. We took our marriage vows seriously.

The truth is, up to that point, neither of us had seen more than 1 or 2 healthy marriages. Our roadmaps were slim to none, and uncharted waters lay ahead. As the years rolled on, each of our sacred vows were thoroughly, sometimes painfully tested when life's seasons changed.

With God's guidance, we have learned new life skills; but still are a serious work in progress.

Our salvation did not take place for over a year after we said, "I do". So, the first year, we did indeed experience rocky times. During our stormy periods, we learned how to live together, forgive each other, and apply God's Word to stay together. *I have refrained my feet from every evil way, that I might keep thy word Psalms 119:101.* It was our commitment to Christ and His Word that caused our marriage to thrive.

After our children were born, the *'for richer and poorer'* seasons made an appearance. Having little to no financial training during those early years, lead to poor money management and debt. As Proverbs 22:7 state, 'The rich rule over the poor and the borrower is slave to the lender'.

The Lord taught us His biblical principles. This forced us to confront our errors and sins in order to make changes in our character. But even in this season, God was faithful. He taught us lessons in faith, frugality, and the meaning of hard work. As long as we faithfully followed the lead of the Holy Ghost, we learned how to navigate difficult situations, over time, but not without pain.

Fast forward to the summer of 2019, we were taking our two grandsons on a mini vacation to northern Michigan to climb Castle Rock and visit Tahquamenon Falls. My wife and I were in pretty good shape. Our workout consisted of walking at least two miles per day coupled with climbing 8-flights of stadium stairs. Climbing the stairs of Castle Rock and taking pictures with our grandsons was something we greatly anticipated.

After taking a brief ferry ride, we began the mile hike to the falls. I (Mark) noticed that my wife was breathing erratically, so we stopped to sit a few times as we approached the falls. When we arrived at Castle Rock, my wife was unable to climb any stairs. We were both greatly concerned about this sudden change.

Upon returning home, we immediately called our daughters to inform them of what had happened. Since all of our three daughters are healthcare workers, they immediately sprang into action and ordered tests to solve this mysterious breathing problem.

The tests revealed that my wife's right lung had completely collapsed. She was admitted into the hospital. After close examination, the doctors concluded that they could find no explanation for the collapsed lung and suggested we take a wait-and-see approach.

After reinflating the lung and draining excess fluid, the doctors suggested, "Come back next year to see if the situation improves on its own." Sad to say, that was very bad advice.

God sent a blessed Christian doctor friend who suggested we see a thoracic specialist immediately to help solve this mystery. We followed his godly advice. We linked our faith and prayed asking the Lord for a good report. The scripture reminds us that He alone will keep us in perfect peace when our minds are stayed on Him (Isaiah 26:3).

We were told that the exploratory surgery would take at least an hour or two. To our surprise, within fifteen or twenty minutes, the mystery was solved. My wife was diagnosed with a very rare form of inoperable stage 4 cancer, with limited time to live. We were devastated.

After 57 years of near perfect health (no smoking, drugs, or drinking), this change was completely unexpected and sent shockwaves to everyone in our family. We never anticipated this type of life changing event to enter our lives.

The enemy, immediately, launched a severe attack against our marriage, family, and spiritual life. These attacks accelerated when there was a sudden hospital stay, painful treatment, or similar period of crisis. The attacks were usually similar: he would bombard our hearts with fear, and dread, or cause us to argue with each other to divide and conquer. The goal of Satan is to kill, steal, and destroy what God has built in our lives (John 10:10 KJV).

To combat this assault, we begin to the use the Word of God as an offensive and defensive weapon. Hebrews 4:12a reads, "For the Word of God is sharper than any two edged sword..." Whenever the enemy came in like a flood in this way, the Holy Spirit would flood our minds with His Word, reminding us of his precious life-giving promises: Rom 8:38-39 reads, "For I am persuaded that neither death, nor life, nor principalities.......would be able to separate me from the love of God in Christ Jesus". He also reminded us that our God is a healer of *all* diseases (Psalms 103: 1 -3 KJV).

The devil was feeding us every evil thought imaginable, but God kept reminding us that "the weapons of our warfare are not carnal, but mighty through God to pull down every stronghold and bring into captivity every thought to the obedience to Christ" (II Corinthians 10:4-6).

After the initial shock, we began to call on the Lord in prayer, filling our thoughts on the healing promises of God 1 Peter 2:24, Isaiah 53:5, Psalms 103:5 to name a few! We even searched out a church that was open during the pandemic that believed in the laying on of hands and casting out of infirmities and every form of sickness. We called on the elders of the church to anoint us with oil. Praying the prayer of faith was essential (James 5: 14-16).

(Sherri) To say that our faith has been tested is an understatement. We know that many are the afflictions of the righteous, but our God is able to deliver us out of them all (Psalms 34:19).

After the initial shock was over, my wife and I went into action! We began to call on the Lord in prayer, filling our thoughts on the healing promises of God; (1 Peter 2:24, Isaiah 53:5, 1 Peter

2:24, Psalms 103:5, 2 Corinthians 10: 3-5) to name a few! We even searched out a church that was open during the pandemic that believed in the laying on of hands and casting out of infirmities and every form of sickness. We called on the elders of the church to anoint us with oil. Praying the prayer of faith was essential, as well (James 5: 14-16).

(Sherri) To say that our faith has been tested is an understatement. We know that many are the afflictions of the righteous, but our God is able to deliver us out of them all (Psalms 34:19).

We did not expect the devastating financial impact that often goes along with a serious illness. In our case, each of the monthly treatments cost $42,000 monthly over a course of 18 months. That was over $700,000 not including doctors' visits, hospital stays, daily medications, and list goes on. We didn't have that kind of money, but the Lord supernaturally provided. The Lord has met every financial conundrum we have faced through this season. Thank you, Lord!

God graced me (Sherri) to stay on my job until I could qualify for retirement which would allow my insurance to cover most costs. It was a mighty struggle! The Lord also provided a program through my Oncologist to pay for a new cutting-edge immunotherapy with no out of pocket costs. We know people who have traveled this journey that have been bankrupted with medical costs, having to choose between medical treatment or paying a mortgage. Thank God that was not our testimony. If you are in this season, be sure to check your medical plans carefully to fully understand your coverage. It is also a good idea to include your doctors in this conversation, they can be a wealth of knowledge and resources. Also reach out to support groups and talk to others who have taken or are currently on this journey.

We have learned during these times of crisis, to examine the depth of our individual faith. It is absolutely critical for each marriage partner to take time alone to process and pour out to the Lord in prayer.

The patient may have times of extreme pain, nausea, and multiple surgeries. Also certain medications can affect your spouse's personality and responses. Expect some irritability from your spouse. Extend lots of patience, understanding and grace, during this season.

Allow your spouse space to process this change of events. Medications will usually come with side-effects that can be very unpleasant. Frustration and bouts of depression can also be expressed during these periods of discomfort.

Allow your spouse to decide how much "help" they require. The supporting spouse should not smother the patient by constant hovering. There is a delicate balance. The key is communication. Ask the patient how you can best serve him or her and then honor their request.

Intently set your heart to hear the Lord. This is a hard season for you both, but remember you are not alone. The Lord has promised to walk with us through these hard places. Allow the tears to flow. My favorite place (Sherri) is sitting in my shower-chair under the flowing warm water. I meet the Lord there, daily, in prayer.

Keep your communication alive! Remember to keep up with date nights, even if date night is spent in bed next to your recovering spouse. Remember the gift of touch is a beautiful way to serve and express your love to your spouse (i.e. back, foot, neck message). Ask your spouse what would be most helpful.

Be open to discuss your sexual relationship in a calm moment. Expect change. A sick spouse may be sexually unavailable for a season. During chemo, after surgeries, inserted catheters and other procedures are often not conducive to sexual intimacy. Also some medications (chemo, etc.) are toxic, and extreme care must be taken to avoid sharing bodily fluids with other members of the household! Seek God's wisdom in this area.

It will be a time to exercise self-control. Your spouse is trying to cope with many things at once. Be sympathetic. Seek to understand each other's heart. Communication, temperance, and compassion are required.

Assist your spouse with his/her self-image, many things may change such as extreme weight loss or weight gain, scarring from surgery, external catheters, external ports, PICC lines, unsightly bandages, the list goes on. Looking in the mirror can be heart-breaking for the patient. But the comfort and encouragement of a loving spouse will bring immense comfort to help adjust to the new changes. Remind your spouse that it is temporary.

Mark helped me change dressings, drain bags and purchase clothes that fit my new frame. His loving words of support, reminding me that I was beautiful in his eyes, gave me the courage I needed to face the outside world. We have experienced all of these things over the past 3 years. It was a slow adjustment, but we have made much progress.

It is important to bring in your support group at this time. Have meals delivered, get help with household chores. Clear your schedule and take time to rest. Sleep as much as possible; the rest helps with healing. Put pride aside and accept the support! Our elderly mother moved in with us for 3 months. Her help was invaluable and appreciated. My flesh however, had to be put under continually, because I was so used to doing everything for myself. Needing extra help takes some getting used to.

The Lord has required mental, spiritual and physical discipline on my (Sherri) part. As my strength returns, I am much more self-sufficient. I am learning about the importance of dietary changes to sustain energy and well-being. I am now able to work-out daily at home. The goal is to build endurance, muscle and lung strength. It's hard work, but it's improving my quality of life. I am determined to do my part during this time of healing. I count everyday as a miracle from the Lord!

Does God heal? Absolutely, but the timetable is His alone. Life is easy, a breeze, when the sun is shining, there is abundance, and everything's coming up roses. It's quite another thing altogether to stand in faith in the midst of a raging life-changing storm.

Each of us will, one day, find ourselves in the valley of the shadow of death, but...Christ has already given us instructions to navigate this foreign land (Psalms 23:4 KJV). Trust the voice of the Holy Spirit to lead you and your spouse through rough waters, and don't surrender your heart to fear. Walk through the valley wearing your full armor (Ephesians 6:11) to deflect the fiery arrows launched by the enemy of your souls. Look unto Jesus who knows our life story from beginning to end (Heb 12:2).

Revisit God's Word as a good soldier must. The alternative is to fall-apart, give way to fear, and ultimately invite the enemy in to wreak havoc in your marriage and life.

Does God allow suffering to enter our lives? Yes. Remember Job. Job was attacked by the enemy in a major way. His wife and friends were no help during his crisis. Job could not see what was taking place in the heavenlies. He was perplexed, covered in boils and sores, and emotionally exhausted. He suffered the loss of his children, his health, his wealth and servants. For Job, this was an evil day; when he traveled the dark road of suffering.

Where was God during Job's distress? Where is He during your times of distress? Right there with you. Do you trust him, really trust him? The scripture said in all his distresses, Job never cursed God or charged him falsely. In other words, through the worst of times, Job's faith did not fail.

When we don't search the scriptures, we will misunderstand who Jesus is. There is a cultural Jesus. This "other Jesus" resembles Santa Clause, or a rich old grandpa. This 'other Jesus' rains down nothing but blessings; and his followers never experience suffering; unlike the multitude of unpleasant life experiences our Christian forefathers endured.

On the contrary, The Jesus of the Bible invites us to take up our cross daily and follow Him (Luke 9:23). In 1 Peter 4:12-13 KJV, it reads:

Beloved, think it not strange concerning the fiery trial which is to try you, as though some strange thing happened unto you: but rejoice, inasmuch as ye are partakers of Christ's sufferings; that, when his glory shall be revealed, ye may be glad also with exceeding joy.

When sickness enters your family equation, you are forced to examine if you are truly in faith when trials come. If we are not rooted and grounded in the whole counsel of the true and living God, we will blame God and allow the enemy to destroy our marriages, and family.

My husband and I are still growing. Our marriage is learning to function on a higher level of prayer and communication. We still battle fear from time to time, but we are learning to war in the spirit instead of with each other. Our prayer life both together and individually is paramount to hearing the voice of the Holy Spirit. I (Sherri) have increased the amount of time I pray in the Holy Ghost exponentially so my spirit can respond to His leading more clearly. I know my God is a healer. He manifests His healing power every day.

Saints, God is faithful. With every life changing turn of this illness, the Lord has provided a way to endure and bear the situation, as we wait for my total healing (1 Cor 10:13). We are overcomers in Christ (John 16:33).

It has been 3 years and counting since my initial diagnosis, and our God does indeed reign. We see the hand of the Lord so clearly as we continue to walk through this season of life. God's healing power is manifesting in so many ways! We are once again walking miles together, but the stairs are a work in progress. One of our goals is to revisit and climb Castle Rock in upper Michigan with our family and take pictures. It will be a personal triumph, to say the least.

Important advice during a health crisis:

1. Don't panic. God is still in control.

2. Develop a more robust prayer life. Expect your faith to be tested.

3. Continue to pay your tithes and offerings in faith!

4. Continue to meet the needs and serve others, when possible.

5. Accept support from family and friends.

6. Seek prayer and oil anointing from the elders of the church.

7. Repent of any unconfessed sin. Give up sinful habits and seek deliverance if necessary.

8. Forgive any and everyone who has offended you.

9. Get to work and do your own research about your diagnosis! Remember, God's part we can't do, our part He won't do.

10. Lighten your load. Eliminate stresses that complicate your life.

11. Seek self-care and alternative treatments.

12. Select the best doctors. Do your research.

13. Research your medical benefits to estimate the financial impact on your family.

Scriptures to meditate on during times of crisis:

Isaiah 40:31 *But they that wait upon the Lord shall renew their strength; they shall mount up with wings as eagles; they shall run, and not be weary; and they shall walk, and not faint.*

Rom 8:37-39 *Nay, in all these things we are more than conquerors through him that loved us. For I am persuaded that neither death, nor life, nor angels, nor principalities, nor powers, nor things present, nor things to come, Nor height, nor depth, nor any other creature, shall be able to separate us from the love of God, which is in Christ Jesus our Lord.*

John 16:33 *These things I have spoken unto you, that in me ye might have peace. In the world ye shall have tribulation: but be of good cheer; I have overcome the world.*

Isaiah 53:5 *But he was wounded for our transgressions, he was bruised for our iniquities: the chastisement of our peace was upon him; and with his stripes we are healed.*

Proverbs 3:5-6 Trust *in the Lord with all thine heart; and lean not unto thine own understanding. In all thy ways acknowledge him, and he shall direct thy paths.*

Bio

Mark and Sherri Bryant have been married for 40 years. They have 3 daughters, Laura, Sara, and Bethany and 4 beautiful grandchildren. They are both teachers by trade. They minister to marriages through their ministry, Lifeline for Today. Currently, the couple reside in West Bloomfield, MI

Contact: Lifeline for Today

Website: Lifelinefortoday.com

Email: Lifelinefortoday@gmail.com

SEVEN

Integrating In-laws

Rene and Maria Aguirre

Refined in the Fire Marriage Ministry

The most important decision you will ever make in your life is to accept Jesus Christ as your personal Savior. The second most important decision you will make, is choosing who you're going to marry and spend the rest of your life with. You get to choose who you want to marry, but you don't get to choose their family, in particular, their parents or siblings, the ones who will become your in-laws.

We don't know what your experience has been or what you've heard, but personally, we believe it is a blessing to have in-laws. Your spouse's parents can be a true blessing, especially if you are young or if you are recently married and trying to figure out how to adjust from being single, child free, without bills or responsibilities other than taking care of yourself. Yes, once you start "adulting" you quickly realize how much your parents were doing for you and how expensive everything is. You may even feel great gratitude towards your parents at this time, and if you do, I strongly suggest you let them know. It can bless them.

All the responsibilities of becoming an adult can feel so overwhelming, so who do you turn to? Naturally, your parents and/or your in-laws are there to offer guidance. And your in-laws will love that!

Even though they know they have done the best they could to raise a responsible young adult, there is something deep down inside every parent's heart that makes them want to hold on to their child. Most don't want to lose their baby! Therefore, many will gladly step in and help in any way they can because they love you and your spouse.

We speak from experience. Twenty-five years ago on our wedding day, my mother (Rene) pulled Maria aside and had the "talk" before going out to do our wedding toast.

I (Maria) remember seeing such profound pain in her eyes. She felt like she was losing her son and may never see him again. She felt no one was going to love him and take care of him the way she did.

My own mother (Maria) had the same love for her children. In her perfect world, all her children would have lived in one big house with their spouses and her grandchildren, all under one roof. "We can be a big happy family!" she would say. She settled for second-best, as I reminded her that all her children and grandchildren were living in California no more than 90 minutes away from her.

And now, we get to experience the other side. Last year our son got married and we became in-laws to his beautiful wife and recently our daughter's husband as well. We were very excited, but also concerned about this new phase of life.

Growing up I heard stories about in-laws from friends and some directly from my brothers and sisters. Most stories were heartwarming; but some were horrifying. The issues are not just about a mother not agreeing with whom their son chose as a wife (which was usually the case). No, these stories were a thousand times worse. And it would make me think, "how can in-laws treat their child's spouse with such hatred and contempt?"

By the time I (Maria) was 9, I was certain I wanted to be a mom when I grew up. At 15, I knew I would someday make a wonderful mom because I loved children so much. I had a lot of practice taking care of my nieces and nephews, but I also aspired to one day be the best mother-in-law possible. I wanted to be one that would love deeply, add value and worth to my kids' relationships, however, I had no idea what that looked like.

What we've seen over the last 12 years since we have been mentoring couples is that differences in cultures and family upbringing have a lot to do with the kind of in-laws we will be. Most of all, a parent's influence in a child's life has a lot to do with the kind of adults, and eventually the kind of in-laws they will turn out to be. So let's go back to the beginning of it all with God's creation of the first marriage.

In Genesis 2:7-25 we read that God created Adam in His own image, made a home for him to live in (Eden), to tend and watch over it. Later, He fashioned Eve out of Adam's rib and brought her to Adam. He performed the very first marriage ceremony and immediately God said to them in verse 24 "For this reason a man shall leave his father and mother and shall cleave (hold fast to, adhere to and be faithfully devoted) to his wife and the two shall become one flesh. (AMP version)

Adam and Eve did not have physical parents like you and I, so that tells us that God was intentional in putting that command there for all future generations and that still applies to us, today. Back then, Adam and Eve were communing with God directly. Today we have access to God thru a relationship with His son, Jesus, and can hold fast to His promises that He will never leave us nor forsake us, and He offers us the Holy Spirit as our helper in this life.

So when we decide to marry, we get to choose our mate, we are supposed to cut ties with our parents and move on to create a family of our own. We need to cut ties physically, financially, and emotionally. However, just like when we are experiencing something for the first time, we need someone we can trust to show us the way, preferably someone who has wisdom and has been thru difficult life experiences, as well. In the Old Testament, we read various stories of older men and women who were in charge of teaching the younger ones valuable life skills. In essence, the kids would be mentored to become husbands/wives, provide for their family, raise children, which in turn would lead them to become in-laws themselves.

We see examples of Moses being mentored by his father-in-law, Jethro. Ruth and Naomi had a special in-law relationship anointed by God. Just like in times past, God entrusts us with children, and it is our responsibility to care and provide for them until they become adults. Then we parent differently. Our parenting is limited to love, encourage, and support. When they marry, we extend our calling to parent the spouse that our children choose, in the same way. We offer respect to our adult children and their spouses.

Not long ago, I remember sitting in the living room where my daughter and her fiancé were having a conversation and making plans for their future, he told my daughter that she was going to make a great wife. She received the compliment with a big smile and said, "I know!" And I (Maria), with a proud look on my face turned towards him and happily added, "You are welcome!"

It is our God-given responsibility to work with our children as best as we can, so they can go out fully prepared to take on this big and challenging world. We shouldn't baby them their entire life and then push them out the door on their 18th birthday, wave and wish them good luck. We also should not let them go out to some mystical place on a self-discovery journey. That can actually be very dangerous. At age 18, they should already know first and foremost, who they are in Christ, that they are loved unconditionally, valued and that they were created with purpose.

Proverbs 22:6 says, "Train up a child in the way they should go and when they are old, they will not depart from it." It is our responsibility to teach and lead our children in the ways of the Lord and help them discover their purpose in life. Let's make this clear, parenting is for a season, being a parent is for a lifetime.

Tips for improving the relationship with your in-laws-

1. Oneness. Remember that you and your spouse are now one, that means forsake all others including your parents, family members and even your own kids. As mentioned earlier, leave, and cleave and become one flesh. **Do not let anyone or anything pull you apart.**

2. Set clear boundaries. Talk with your spouse on how involved both of your parents will be in your life, how you will spend the holidays, how the grandkids should be cared for when spending time with them.

3. You are your own entity. From the day you said, "I do", you are no longer attached to your parents. Cut the umbilical cord. Start your own life in your own home with your own rules and traditions. Some traditions you will decide to adopt from your parents and some you will come up with as a couple.

4. Do not air out your dirty laundry. Issues between a couple should be discussed with a marriage mentor or a licensed therapist. Venting or seeking help from your in-laws, family members or friends can cause deep resentment towards your spouse and division after you resolve your issues.

5. Ignore the little things. Choose your battles with your in-laws. Don't stress over the little things that won't matter in a few weeks or a few years.

6. Don't budge on the big things. Things that are very important to you and you're not willing to compromise.

7. Don't assume your in-laws understand your convictions. Consider their religious beliefs, their upbringing, and their culture.

8. Give your in-laws a chance to learn and grow. Explain lovingly why you feel so strong about a certain subject and the reason for doing things differently.

9. Love them where they are. Remember, love covers a multitude of sin.

10. Love from a distance. If you can't seem to see eye to eye with your in-laws, respect them, be cordial, pray for God to heal your relationship and love them.

11. Caring for elderly parents. Expect the unexpected, as our parents get older, they may need your assistance. If they ever need to move in with you, the same rules apply. Maintain oneness at all costs, set clear boundaries, love and respect your parents/in-laws, and if they try to "help" by giving you marriage advice or tell you how to raise your kids, remember that they are only giving you their well-intentioned advice. You can take it or leave it, but lovingly let them know that you appreciate them just the same.

I now understand Psalm 127:4 it says "Like arrows in the hand of a warrior, so are children of one's youth."

Arrows need a bow (parents) in order to be launched, and they have a target (purpose). Arrows are pulled back; tension is applied on them (life's troubles) but at the right time they are released to hit their mark. If we don't invest in our children's lives and pour into them, it will be difficult for them to fulfill God's purpose and plan for their lives. I'm going to say it again-parenting is only for a season, but being a parent is for a lifetime.

So, what is an appropriate age to start training a child to become a husband or a wife? And what is the right way to do that? Well, we are not experts in parenting and have not done everything perfectly, but this is what worked for us. I began with turning to God and trusting Him. I (Maria) gave my life to the Lord at the age of 27, I (Rene) gave my life at 37. Since then our eyes have been opened to God's truth and we continue to gain wisdom thru His Word, the Bible.

We have been married for 25 years, we are a blended family, we have 3 children, and our 3rd grandchild is on her way. Together we decided to raise all 3 kids with biblical principles and found out it's never too late to teach and correct with God's word. Our son was already a teenager at the time we took on this approach and a lot of the things we had told him before could now be backed up according to the Bible. So this is the pattern we lived by. It worked well for us, and it can help you too.

Tips for raising children-

So from 0-5 years old we need to get control of our children, establish, and exercise our authority in the home. In this phase, we teach and discipline. I know some parents have different opinions when it comes to spankings as a form of discipline. We frequently used time outs. However, we did not hold back on spanking; as long as it was done after praying, with love, and not in the heat of the moment. Spankings were rare; but, when the time called for it, our children always knew exactly why they were getting spanked. This helped us minimize embarrassing tantrums while we were out shopping or trying to have a nice family dinner. We also found out that giving a warning by counting to 3 does not work. I wanted to be able to give a command and train them to comply the first time. During this phase, we often referred to Ephesians 6:1 which says "Children, obey your parents in the Lord, for this is right."

From 6-12 years old, we train the child and model Christlike behavior to instill godly values in them. We start assigning responsibilities accordingly, like cleaning up their toys, choosing their outfit for school, brushing their hair and teeth. And... speaking of teeth, I have a great story to tell; My daughter Jessica was about 10 years old when she got tired of me reminding her to brush her teeth every night. Her little sister Nicole was 7, and she also requested the same privilege. Every so often I would ask if they had brushed their teeth and I would always get a "Yes momma" as a response from both. Even then, I would go check their toothbrushes and they were wet, so I would go to bed feeling accomplished. After about five months of following this routine, I took the girls for a regular dental cleaning. I was shocked when the dentist wanted to talk to me privately to ask if everything was ok at home. I said, "Yes, of course! But, why?" And she said, "Because Jessica has 11 cavities." My jaw immediately dropped, and I was afraid to ask about Nicole, but I went for it. Thankfully, Nicole only had 1 cavity. So you can imagine the conversations we had and the consequences that followed. It turned out Nicole was brushing her teeth every night; but Jessica thought she would outsmart me and was only wetting her toothbrush every night. Gross!!!

From 13-18 years old we coach, and just as a coach shows a child how to kick a soccer ball, and then lets the child try it, we are to do the same. We can make corrections as needed until the child can do it all on his/her own. At this point, we start entrusting them with more responsibilities and allowing them to reap the benefits or face the consequences of their choices.

At 19 + we become their consultants and give advice if solicited. We have been diligent, put in the hard work and now we can watch our children practice being grown-ups. If they have moved out of the home, they don't need to follow their parents' rules anymore. However, they are still called by the Lord to respect their parents. Yet there is a caveat; if they are still dependent on parents to give them money and/or provide a roof over their heads, then they should still obey the head of household and their rules. The second part of Ephesians 6:4 says "Honor your father and mother which is the first commandment with a promise, so that it may go well with you and that you may enjoy long life on the earth.

I believe if we follow the steps above, our children will be ready to be launched into the world, well prepared for marriage, ready to manage the different types of relationships with friend, co-workers, a boss and including the one with their in-laws.

Bio

We are Rene and Maria Aguirre, founders of Refined in the Fire Ministries. Our ministry includes sharing God's heart for marriage and relationships through Biblical mentoring.

We passionately seek to help make marriages whole in God's power. We mentor, train, teach and disciple believers and non-believers alike from the Word of God. Our aim is to help them understand their true identity in Jesus Christ, so that they can have powerful relationships, which result in life giving marriages.

We are intimately familiar with a marriage focused on the principles of the world, the sting, heartbreak and pain from unhealthy relationships, and the deep-rooted hope and joy of a fully restored marriage centered on Jesus Christ. It is this unique perspective and experience that we obediently share in private as we meet with couples, individuals and with whomever would benefit from our testimony. We are a blended family that have been married over 25 years and have 3 wonderful children ages 30, 24 and 21 and we also have 3 beautiful grandchildren.

We are not licensed counselors or psychotherapists, but marriage mentors ordained by God. We have been serving the Lord in marriage ministry over 12 years.

Contact: Refined in the Fire

Email: refinedinthefire.2@gmail.com

Phone: 925-433-7808

Website: www.refinedinthefireministries.com

EIGHT

Overcoming Pornography by Covenant Collaboration

Gregory and Saryta Colbert

Dare to Thrive Ministries

In the distance was the faint sound of clanking metal and the whisper of chains jangling. As the people of Israel stood straining to recognize the inharmonious sounds, a darkening cloud of dust overwhelmed them as the warriors of Amalek descended upon them. Fear seized the hearts of God's chosen people and without hesitation, Moses commanded Joshua to band together an army of men to go out and fight the army of Amalek for them. As the fierce battle between two nations waged, Moses knew that overcoming this threat would require a need for divine intervention in the midst of the battle. Along with his companions, Aaron and Hur, Moses stood on the top of a hill overlooking the conflict with staff in hand. In a grand "Red Sea-like" sweeping motion, Moses held up the staff in his hand. The tide quickly turned, and the Israelites gained the advantage. Moses remained steadfast and immovable supporting the battle behind the scenes, pursuing victory in prayer with the uplifted staff. The fate of Israel in this battle depended upon his intervention. When he prayed Israel prevailed and when he stopped praying Amalek prevailed. But to his dismay, the weight of supporting the battle in this manner was unmanageable alone and Moses could not easily continue. Purposefully positioned, Aaron and Hur came alongside Moses placing a large rock underneath him to recline against and each one of them held his hands up as support in prayer. They partnered with him in a moment where his own strength was failing him. This partnership was the prevailing force that made Moses' efforts successful: his hands remained steady until the going down of the sun. The people of Israel claimed the victory. (Exodus 17)

You're probably asking, what in the world does this story have to do with pornography? We are so glad you asked. Israel's victory over the Amalekites was a result of purposeful collaboration. Without the collaboration of Moses, Aaron, Hur, Joshua, and the Israelite soldiers, a victory that was designed for Israel would have ended in defeat. Not because they didn't have God's blessing! They would have been defeated because of a lack of collaboration. The foundation of transformation is often times found in the power of teaming up. We see this throughout the Bible. Jesus collaborated with 12 disciples in order for the message of Christ to be spread throughout the world. Divinity collaborated with humanity to see the redemption of the world.

Woven into the fabric of scripture is the undeniable power of working together. But if we are able to draw out the obvious power of collaboration, it would be unwise to assume that our enemy is not well aware of this principle. Satan is a master student of all things that can bring glory to God. It then would be imperative for us to note that there is only one entity used according to God as a reflection of his relationship with the church and that covenant is called marriage. *So we could safely say that the ultimate earthly collaboration after our collaboration with God is the collaboration between a husband and wife.* With this as a backdrop, it then should bring clarity to the challenges spouses experience in marriage. The enemy's goal is to prevent collaboration. And one of the ways the enemy accomplishes this is through the weapon called pornography.

We could get into the statistics of how many marriages are negatively affected by pornography; but we believe it's safe to say that this weapon has left many marriages hurt, bleeding and lifeless. It has left homes in ruins; trust in shambles; children broken and led many marriages to divorce. Pornography is a multi-faceted weapon that seeps into so many other areas of life and has the capacity to affect everything, from your finances to your mental health to your employment. It is a leech that will not be satisfied until it kills, steals, and destroys everything that resembles the image of God we are to bare. The enemy uses this weapon to encourage couples to turn on each other, to assign blame, to accuse one another. The enemy uses pornography to create separation; not only physically, but in spirit and emotions, which ultimately leads to division. This distracts us from the real enemy.

Just for sobering clarity, it is not your spouse. I'll say that again for the people in the back...

Your enemy is *not* your spouse!

Our goal in this chapter is to identify the responsibility of each spouse and how to work together to overcome this weapon the enemy uses to prevent the impact your marriage was designed and destined to have! There are two positions that you may find yourself occupying when it comes to porn. The **Responsible Spouse** that has engaged in pornographic activity and the **Restorative Spouse** that has been equipped by God to support their spouse on the journey to freedom. Let's start with the Responsible Spouse.

Responsible Spouse

I know what it's like to be in this position. I found myself falling into the trap of believing that once I got married and could "get some" any time I wanted; the desire for porn would no longer be present. I was deceived, only to find myself within the first year of marriage watching porn more than I would like to admit. What I didn't realize is that the spirit of lust needs to be satisfied and after I said, "I do" to my spouse, lust needed a new way to be fulfilled. Because marriage is not designed to provide deliverance from sexual addiction or healing from sexual trauma.

I had no idea the price tag and how much it would cost to get free. I am happy to say today that I am free. Now when I say free, I don't mean that I don't ever deal with temptation. When I say free, I mean I am no longer controlled by or a slave to pornography. It doesn't consume my every thought and it has lost its attraction or pull in my mind and heart. I am free in both areas and man does it feel good. I want to share 5 keys that I found to be my road map to freedom.

1. Repent

One of the Biblical definitions of repent is to have a change of mind. This change of mind is only the result of superior exposure. We usually don't see the need to change until something better is presented and then admitting that our current way is ultimately inferior to divine design.

I first had to understand before I ever broke my spouse's heart, I had broken God's heart. I had to remember I am a child of God before I am a spouse. It is only when I could truly repent before

God that I was able to offer true repentance to my spouse. True repentance is accompanied by brokenness. When we don't really believe we are wrong, our awareness for grace isn't apparent. It is only in the depth of our brokenness that we get to truly experience the depth of God's love and grace accompanied by the depth of love and grace that a covenant-minded spouse is committed to. If I were to give a final directive, true repentance is responsible to be accountable to all parties that have been affected by our inferior behavior.

2. Renew

Once I completed the process of repentance the next step was mind renewal. Good intentions without clear corresponding actions lead to empty promises. I didn't want to be that person any longer; but my desire alone fell flat in the face of an addiction that had more of my time and devotion than my pursuit of freedom had. According to Paul, transformation is the result of mind renewal. It is the process of not only introducing superior thoughts to our way of thinking but it is also the eviction of inferior thoughts that has kept the vicious cycle of returning to the addiction. (Romans 12:2 NKJV)

I looked up every scripture in the Bible that dealt with lust, sexual immorality, and the flesh. Every day for a year, I read those scriptures. When temptation came, I found I was now equipped to fight temptation with The Word instead of my desire to be free. I watched messages and read books that strengthened my faith in the area of overcoming lust. This new approach to freedom created new habits that supported my new way of thinking and ultimately changed my behavior which led to the power to break cycles and walk in freedom.

3. Regain

If there was a mission statement for the enemy in the Bible it would come from John 10:10 NKJV "'The thief does not come except to steal, and to kill, and to destroy...'" Oftentimes, we're quick to celebrate the survival of a hard season; but we fail to pause and take an assessment of what was lost during that season. Every season isn't a "kill" season, sometimes the enemy's goal is to steal something from you. When it came to lust, I came to realize that not only had my spouse lost trust and confidence in me, but I had also lost trust and confidence in myself. I needed to rebuild trust by giving my spouse a greater level of access to my ungodly desires as well as my devices. During that season, I had to allow my spouse to have all passwords to all devices and accounts. I gave my spouse the authority to determine my social media interactions and the freedom to ask difficult and uncomfortable questions. I did my best to refrain from offense, understanding that this was the harvest of the seeds I had sown for years; and I would need to move forward *at the pace of my spouse's healing*. Yes, this was all necessary. However, what I wasn't expecting was my ability to remain committed to this process was the means in which God used to help me prove to myself that I was capable of being trusted again. It was my submission to the process that became the foundation of restored confidence.

4. Relay

I have spoken to countless individuals about overcoming lust and there is never a time that I don't stress the need for accountability. The lack of accountability is the number one thing the enemy will attempt to use to keep us from embracing freedom, with shame being the motivator. The reason many of us don't get free from pornography is that to admit it would open us up to the strong possibility of being shamed. Not by God, but by people. We don't want to be looked at differently. We don't want people to know we struggle in that way. We are sometimes unwilling to damage our reputation. What I had to realize on my journey is that my bondage was being funded by my pride, and the only way to break the back of pornography and shame was by committing to a life of humility.

My wife told me that my sin would continue to gain power in the darkness, but if I was willing to light it up, drag it into the light and expose it, it would lose its power. I honestly pushed back from this advice because that would mean frequently having to admit I wasn't as well put together as many thought I was…and maybe what I told myself. I kid you not, every time I took this advice and brought it to the light, I felt the power of the enemy lose its grip and I felt stronger than ever before.

The power of sin lies in its secrecy and freedom is on the other side of confession. Not only when you fall but when the very temptation comes calling for you to reconnect with your bondage. This takes courage and it takes humility, but God said He would give grace to the humble. That grace is God's empowerment and it's waiting for you and me to embrace it and light it up.

5. Repel

After I walked through these 4 steps, I had to evaluate what the historic open doors were that the enemy used to gain access to my mind. I had to identify the triggers and my own desires that drew me away from righteousness. I realized that staying up late without my spouse was a trigger. I realized sexual rejection from my spouse was a trigger. I realized that when my spouse was disrespectful and lashed out in anger was a trigger. Watching movies that had sex scenes, nudity and excessive sexuality were all open doors. I had to evaluate each of these and come up with a plan that I communicated with my spouse to intentionally combat these temptations. I could not overly expose my freedom to bondage nostalgia. My freedom was too precious to me to expose it to the harsh dynamics of sexual perversion. I had to create safeguards and boundaries to shift my behaviors and change the level of access the enemy had to me.

Guarding your eye gates and your ear gates must become your obsession! Then and only then will you be able to resist the devil. He has studied you for years and you must interrupt your predictability with new behaviors that are from the Word of God that are designed to overcome the weapons of the enemy.

Restorative Spouse

"Two people are better off than one, for they can help each other succeed. If one person falls, the other can reach out and help. But someone who falls alone is in real trouble."

Ecclesiastes 4:9-10 NLT

God in all His infinite wisdom and phenomenal cosmic power knew it to be absolutely necessary to put this scripture in the Bible. He knew that without it, we may come to believe that we are independent beings without the need of purposeful partnerships to aid us in times of conflict, crisis, and trauma.

But He knew having the ability to restore health, strength, or a feeling of well-being to a broken relationship would not be lasting simply at the hand of the offender.

As we have seen above, there are necessary steps that the Responsible Spouse must take in order to reconcile what has been broken by the sledgehammer of lust and pornography. Putting the broken pieces of the marriage, as well as themselves, back together come at a cost and take time, intentionality, ownership, and resilience.

And who we like to affectionately call, the Restorative Spouse, plays a huge part in working alongside the Responsible Spouse. They work together putting the focus on repairing the harm that has been done to their marriage relationship. In the same way that the Responsible Spouse must walk through a process that leads to freedom, the Restorative Spouse must also walk through a process that leads to healing. I want to share 5 keys that supported my (Saryta) healing journey and lead to a beautiful love story.

1. Remember

"I do" are probably the most popular words at a wedding. While "I do" gets all the attention, the vows surrounding "I do" seem to get lost in the sea of celebration of the response of the eager bride and groom. I remember looking into the eyes of my spouse promising to love him in sickness and health, for richer or poorer, for better or worse, until death do us part. I also remember looking into the eyes of my spouse when what some would deem *the worst* was happening to me. This was the moment when my vows came knocking, requiring a response of "come in" instead of "no one's home." I had a choice to make. Would I uphold the law of a contract or the love of a covenant?

Contractually speaking, if one party doesn't hold up their end of the agreement, the contract can be broken. This is not the way in the kingdom of God. In marriage, God creates a covenant between both parties and Himself. This is not nullified by one party's lack of follow through on that commitment. In other words, if my spouse is not performing their part of the agreement, I must remember I am more committed to my God and my covenant than to my spouse. I must live out my part with passion and commitment even in the absence of reciprocation. Marriage will never be short of the opportunity to remember covenant.

2. Respond

Transparent moment... this is the place I struggled the most. When a trauma like lust or pornography are the poison of choice, will your emotional immune system be able to withstand the attack? Our emotions are a powerful force to be reckoned with. Not managed correctly, they can leave insurmountable damage in the wake of their blow. The difficulty is when we're convinced our emotional response is justified because of the weight of the offense.

I remember the tears, the yelling, the belittling, and the name calling that ensued after my spouse shared his most vulnerable secret. This response may have been authentic, but it was not edifying. Jesus was the greatest example of responding with not only truth, but also grace. There was a particular woman in the Bible that was caught in the act of adultery. She was brought before the people in an effort to have her answer for her crime. Jesus had every right according to the law to have this woman stoned, but His response highlighted the proper position of the heart "He who is without sin cast the first stone. (John 8:7 KJV)" Whenever our spouse makes a mistake it is appropriate to communicate the pain that it caused. But we must not allow our emotions to dictate a lack of honor and respect for our spouse. Our emotions should indicate a need for God and His grace that says I, too, have needed and will continue to need the same grace that my spouse currently needs.

3. Reassure

Reassurance is a healing balm that soothes an anxious heart, especially in moments of trauma. It requires the Restorative Spouse to step outside of the trauma and to see with eyes filled with faith, hope and love. Reassurance is the verbal bridge that fills the gap between doubt and truth. Without it, we are subject to fill our gaps with suspicion.

The Restorative Spouse must do the humbling work of assuring the Responsible Spouse that they are committed to the healing process. This healing journey is a road both spouses must travel. As we both pursued the growth and recovery necessary to lead to a greater level of intimacy, our companionship on this journey spoke the healing words "you are not alone." It is in the same manner that God spoke the words in Deuteronomy 31:8 NKJV, "I will never leave or forsake you," that keeps our hearts assured of His unfailing love. Our presence on this journey with our spouse is picturesque of that very same love.

4. Rewrite

Trauma has a way of calling our identity into question. It can leave us feeling stripped of the truth and confidence of who we once believed we were. We find ourselves questioning every decision we made leading up to the point of trauma, picking it apart in an attempt to find the place where things went wrong. We ask questions like, "How did I miss this?" "Is there something wrong with me?" Or we assign guilt by telling ourselves "I knew something wasn't right, if only I had..." Trauma does not reassign truth.

When I found out that my spouse was struggling with pornography, the impact of this trauma left me dazed and confused. My emotions didn't know which way was up. The trauma attempted to dictate a new narrative. Was I not enough? Did he still love me? What did these other women have that I didn't? Will he struggle with this forever? With time, prayer, and counsel, I came to realize the truth of who I am is not based on what has happened to me or what I have been through. My truth is based on the One who is the Truth and what He says is true. God had to restore the narrative. He reminded me that I am enough, that I am loved, and that the uniqueness of my womanhood was fearfully and wonderfully made (Psalms 139:14 NKJV). I also needed to rewrite the narrative of my spouse. Words like nasty, pervert, cheater, and deceiver filled the pages of my mind. And just like the master editor He is, God reminded me of the truth about my spouse, that he was not a sinful person pursuing after righteousness, but a righteous person pursuing after the things of God. Trauma doesn't reassign truth, but Truth reassigns your trauma.

5. Rely

Many spouses attempt to keep the communication surrounding the hurt and pain they have experienced from each other between themselves. I quickly understood that I needed healthy avenues to share my hurt and pain. The qualifications of these individuals were very specific: They could not be emotionally vulnerable; They needed to be free of any biases, having a commitment to the marriage and not one individual spouse. They needed to share my value for marriage and the importance of covenant.

This group was made of individuals that were able to meet different needs. I had a mentor, a person that was further along than I was, who had obtained wisdom that I was pursuing. I had a peer group that was agreed upon between me and my spouse as a place I could seek comfort and support while sometimes just needing to vent. My journal was the place I could record my pitfalls, progress, and pivots. Most importantly, my conversations with God, the One I could run to above all else. The reliance on these outlets provided me the means to keep my heart empty of offense, but full of hope and focused on healing.

"Walk with the wise and become wise, for a companion of fools suffers harm."

Proverbs 13:20 NIV

Together

As we close this chapter, we would like to shift the focus from your marriage to Christ's marriage to the church. Jesus died well aware that we would sin and fall short, but He also died *knowing* we would be repeat offenders! He *knew* this and never lacked in zeal and passion to reconcile us to the Father. Our prayer is that you never lack in zeal and passion to see your spouse walk in freedom and you walk in healing. The good news is that we overcome by the blood of the Lamb and the words of our testimonies (Revelation 12:11 KJV). God is depending on your marriage testimony to be a prophecy of hope for marriages in the future. We can't wait to hear how God uses what the enemy meant for bad, for your good and the good of others!

Bio

Greg and Saryta Colbert have been married for 17 years and have served in ministry for over 16 years together. During this time they have always put an emphasis on their first ministry; the Colbert Crew. They have been blessed to have 4 children. Over the years they have served in multiple ministry roles as Children's Pastor, Youth Pastor, Young Adult Pastor, Assistant Pastor, and Worship Director. In 2007, they received their first assignment to Pastor a church that met in a seniors' facility in Pittsburg, Ca. This opportunity led to them planting New Life Church in 2009 where they served for 4 years as the Senior Pastors. After 4 years of serving New Life Church, they were led to move to the Phoenix, AZ area in 2013. Soon after relocating, they started an event for marriages and singles entitled, Love, Sex, and Relation-Tips. This event gave people the opportunity to invest in their current relationship season. The heart of the event was summed up in one simple phrase "God's way is not just right, it's better!" Seeing the growing need in the area of relationships they started a ministry called Decide to Thrive. D2T exists to raise the standard of relationships and equip singles, marriages, and families to leave a thriving legacy. D2T has hosted relationship seminars, provided relationship coaching, and has recently released its first book entitled rethink reLATIONSHIPS. Currently, Greg and Saryta are full-time staff members at Faith Christian Center in Phoenix, AZ under the leadership of Pastor Sean and Erica Moore. Greg serves as the Youth Minister and Worship Director and Saryta serves as the Children's Director. They also partner together as the Young Adult Pastors at the church as well. Their life and family mission are to live life in such a way that people would see the fruit of their lives and want to experience the God they serve.

Contact: Decide 2 Thrive

Website: www.decidetothrive.org

Email: decidedtothrivellc@gmail.com

Phone: 602.521.2492

FB: www.Facebook.com/WeD2T

IG: we_d2t

NINE

Overcommitment

Oscar & Crystal Jones

Marriage for a Lifetime Ministries

Exhausted, short-tempered and nearly burned-out is how many of today's couples find themselves. As young professionals, they pack their schedules with too many activities to count, including a plethora of activities for their children. These well-meaning couples find themselves emotionally bankrupt with little energy left at the end of the day. Unfortunately, their marriage is left on cruise control with no intentional effort, leaving everyone edgy and disconnected.

In our fast-paced, high-demand culture, overcommitment is seen as a measure of success. It is unfortunate that we prioritize so many other things over our relationships.

We all get 168 hours in a week. Fifty-six of those hours are assigned for sleep. Subtract another 40 hours for work. That leaves us a whopping 72 hours per week. But there is a limit as to how much activity you can stuff in that time period. There has to be time set aside for relationships and rest.

Some families try to compensate by taking hours away from sleep. It keeps life moving at a supersonic speed. Couples often find themselves passing each other by on the way to something else. In most cases, they are also neglecting their time with God, leaving everything out of order.

They often have to pay for things they would normally do themselves (Uber, Door Dash, Instacart, etc.). So families are paying out more money than they anticipated. The house is in disarray, dirty laundry is mounting, and they find themselves eating take out more than desired. If everyone in the family is depleted, how will the household tasks get done?

We can't take on unlimited commitments. It's like spending more money than you have in the bank. You will find yourself bankrupt. At some point, we have to pause to evaluate if we have room to add another commitment. And if we think we do, is this *'the one'* that needs to be added? Everything that sounds good isn't.

Overcommitment is sacrificing the sacred for something lesser. Early in our marriage, I, Crystal, worked 1 full time job and 1 part-time job. I was studying for my bachelor's degree in business administration while also attending Real Estate school. My husband was working on his master's degree and was teaching full time, as well. So we didn't see much of each other. It was way too much for a young family. I remember coming home late from one job after the girls went to bed and leaving early in the morning before they went to school. My girls (ages 3 and 4 at the time) asked my husband, "Did Mommy go on a vacation?" That was a crushing reality check for me. I was doing too much, and it was affecting my children. We needed to make major adjustments in our schedules. Trying to achieve a certain standard of living wasn't worth what we were giving up. I realized that no amount of success was more important than my husband and children.

We were sacrificing things that were irreplaceable to have what the culture said was better. Often families are trying to keep up with the proverbial Joneses. The price is just too high.

The children of millennials are just as busy as their parents. Studies show our kids are more stressed than previous generations. They are hard pressed to keep up with the pace of their peers. Class work, technology, sports, band, afterschool activities, school plays, social clubs and navigating family issues is a lot to juggle. Let us pause, reflect, and not pass on our bad habits to our children.

We have to ask ourselves what are our core values and what matters most to us? When your chapter ends on this earth, will you wish you had worked more hours? Probably not. Most people will regret not spending more time with those they loved.

Foundational to all marriages and families is how we spend our time. Couples have to *make time* for one another, not try to find it. Trying to find time is an almost impossible task. Because we've set other things that we are unwilling to move. Making excuses for why we can't spend time with our spouse and/or children it is a bad sign that our priorities are not as they should be.

Couples would do well by setting up a weekly date night and a weekly family night. These little adjustments help the marriage and family stay on track.

Here are some practical tips to avoid overcommitment.

1. Pray and listen. Ask God for direction. Everything you do is not for this season. Be open to changing your plans, if necessary. Follow the Lord who is keenly aware of our limitations (Ps 103:13-14).

2. Set up Sabbath time to breathe and rest. Don't feel guilty about resting. It is a healthy practice. The Bible encourages it (Mark 2:27-28).

3. Keep up with your date nights. Don't cancel. If there is a dire emergency that you have to attend to than reschedule; but don't make a habit of skipping your date

nights. You need to reconnect with your spouse regularly. Commit to giving each other one day out of 7 (Proverbs 5:18)

4. Plan family time. Many families find that Sundays work best. Set aside one day out of the week to play board games, create an art project, go to the park, have a dance competition, *do* something together as a family. Connect with your children. They will be gone before you know it.

Even if you find yourself already overextended, you can still change the way things are going to get your priorities back in alignment. Sit down with your spouse and pray for God's guidance. Take everything off the schedule and start from scratch. Start adding things back in the order of importance. You've got this one life on this earth to get it right. Let's give it our best shot.

TEN
Tug of War: Power Struggles

Ron & LaShun Franklin

Song of Solomon Relationship Institute

What is the one word that comes to mind when you think of the following words: control, power, influence, authority, leadership, leader, money, sex, submission, agreement, win or lose? Is it possible that "marriage" was not the first word that came to mind? Maybe you thought of career, politics or success, first. Unfortunately, these very powerful words play out in some marriages almost daily, with the ability to destroy a loving relationship.

What is power and what is a power struggle? In a relationship, power refers to that one who holds the leverage, influence or authority in one area or another. If you add in control, then it becomes significantly more ominous. Power and control would seem to mean that there is a very deliberate intent to express dominance in the relationship. Now, bear with us for a moment. In a marriage where power and control may be an issue, then there may also be a struggle, meaning that the other spouse is fighting for their power or control, also. This struggle may not be as deliberate or conscious for either spouse, however it plays a huge role in the health and well-being of the marriage, and it must be acknowledged.

It all started back in 1991, the year we wed. The "I Do's" were over and we were snuggled into our first apartment. Things seemed to be going very well for a good little while... until it wasn't. We acquiesced to most requests and were very flexible with our differences, even making jokes or poking fun at one another. After a year, those small preferences or differences became major disagreements. We began to fight over things like how one 'should' or 'should not' squeeze the toothpaste container or leaving the toilet seat up or down. We even argued over the amount of closet or drawer space each of us deserved! We managed to pretend to get through these small issues, until the birth of our daughter 3 ½ years later. That is when the powder keg exploded!

Bringing a child into the world is a very life changing experience. As beautiful and precious as it is, it tested the very fabric of who we are as a couple. Those were the times where our individual pasts and the way we were parented collided. Our true beliefs about life, religion, discipline, and structure surfaced in a very dogmatic way. The 'his way-her way' dance began and neither one of us was bound to lose!

Ron was the eldest of 5 boys and LaShun was an only child and the eldest of the grandchildren. The birth order paradox with the only child syndrome and oldest squared up for control. Ron loved living free style and LaShun lived by principles and order. Within these paradigms, our power and control issues were undeniable. When it came to things being done 'right' and orderly, LaShun would hold fast to the principles that she was taught or those she caught from her family. Ron was more of an inspirational person, if it feels good or acceptable then go with it. The routines were challenging, and the money was even a greater challenge! Due to the lack of negotiation skills and communication, it was very difficult to find places of agreement.

We were constantly battling over minor things and those things turned into major issues. The underlying feelings or themes that drove each of our behaviors surfaced as: "I won't be controlled by you" and "I am valuable". The narratives and self-talk that we engaged in led us to believe that if we gave into the other's will, then we were 'less-than' or weak. Both of these thought patterns bubbled up to the surface of our marriage from events in our childhoods. The abuse, belittling, bullying and dismissiveness of our pasts, led us to believe that we had to fight each other to gain dominance over those memories or voices. The areas that we felt we had no control over as children and young adults, drove us to gain control and power over as a spouse. We used our marriage as the battleground for our negative beliefs. In those years that followed, sex, communication and trust were impacted so severely that our feelings of love were crippled. Disrespect and neglect became a common scenario as we tried to figure out how to *submit one to another out of our reverence for Christ* as Ephesians 5:20-21 tells us to do. We realized that though we were Christians and regularly did our religious duties, we had somehow kicked Christ out of our marriage. It wasn't intentional. We allowed our fears of being controlled and dominated by one another to take priority over the love, surrender, and Christian character that we were supposed to be demonstrating, daily.

How did we overcome the power struggle? Well, it absolutely took some real prayer, effort, knowledge/skill, and accountability. Our change in this area began with the revelation that we were fighting each other and not dealing with the mindsets that had us both deceived. When we were exposed to marriage conferences and couples working on their marriages, things began to open for us.

It's sad to admit, that the power-struggle even continued in prayer. One year, we attended a marriage conference and were asked to pray together out loud! Novel idea, right? However, this request was very challenging for us. It was habit for us to say the grace or blessing over our food, and we prayed for protection when we left home, but really praying **together** was a whole different experience. We had tried praying together before, it resulted in fights afterwards! Each of us tried to play the victim with God, who knew our issues. We wanted God to see the other's faults and make ourselves look innocent. Once we learned to pray **for** one another instead of **about** one another, each of our attitudes began to shift. God gave us compassion for the other where we were able to sense and respond to needs and hurts appropriately. This was the breaking up of our hardened hearts and it began with prayer. There is an old saying that prayer is the key that unlocks the door, and this was true for the Franklins.

Similarly, faith, without corresponding action is useless. The healing of our marriage took more than prayer! It took intentional effort on both parts, and that required humility. We had to get rid of the 50/50 mentality that we came into the marriage with. We began to put the work in and not expect our issues to change because we wanted our way. God allowed us to come across some life-changing materials and books that helped us get healthy. We learned about ourselves and one another and began to search the scriptures for answers. When we learned something, we attempted to put it into action. Many of the principles that we learned, went against what we 'caught' from the relationships around us and the cultural norms that we were subjected to at the time. Pushing through those barriers was tough, because it took abandoning stubbornness, worldly ideology and culture. We knew that success could come if God was the One in control of our marriage. We needed to hear His heart.

Proverbs chapter 3 begins with an admonishment to trust in God and don't just depend on our understanding of things. We knew this scripture and had it memorized. However, it impacted us more when we began to live it. There was not just a power struggle going on with us as a couple, but within us as individuals. We found that we were both very strong willed. And we needed to submit our wills to the Lord.

The breaking began with prayer; and then God giving us the desire to "want" what He wanted. We were building on something. Light was coming, but we needed some skills to maintain our healing process. We had to seek out help and learn some tools that would forever be a part of our arsenal to fight culture and the enemy of our marriage! In 2 Peter 1:5, we are encouraged to not to stop at just believing, but to build on our basic faith and add important things like character, knowledge, self-control, discipline, godliness and affection for others. We had to learn some things and then develop a consistency in using the tools we gained. This was a game-changer! Reading books, going to conferences, and using what we learned daily was key to our success in overcoming the power and control. Get wisdom and skill and apply it.

The temptation to continue to fight and assert our will over the other did not cease, even after gaining prayer, action and knowledge. The Franklins needed accountability! Our habit was to have a nice stretch of time where we did well and things were good, only to get caught in our crazy cycle after an incident. We felt bad and sometimes wondered if we could actually break the cycle.

During one of our marriage retreats, God spoke to us and told us that we needed accountability. We needed like-minded people, who were as passionate about marriage as we were to come along side of us and hold us both accountable for our actions (or lack of action). Though we were surrounded by a team of amazing couples, we had to pray and ask God for the right couple, who had the boldness and the biblical foundation to become what we needed. God highlighted 2 couples that fit the description. This request was one that required more humility and intention, and we jumped in! It was the best thing that we added as a pillar in our lives. We set regular check-ins with them, prayed with them, and took some of our hard decisions to the table to get wisdom and to check the flesh. As we said earlier, many of our issues came from our past. We were not willing to continue to sweep them under the rug. Counseling was then integrated into our lifestyles as a form of accountability to ourselves and our future. Putting all of these elements in place and sticking to them has been infectious and now we teach everyone who is willing to listen, to do them intentionally.

We want to encourage all of those who are reading this chapter with this: There is nothing impossible to the couple who chooses to believe that they can operate in peace and unity. It's not about how fast you change or how significant the sacrifice, it's about pleasing God, being humble and being intentional about the health and welfare of your marriage. Giving up is not an option (especially the only option). If God could help us and deliver us from the constant cycle of power, control, neglect and even abuse of one another, then He can help You! We were not special, nor did we have great examples to follow. We were just determined not to give up or allow the Evil One to destroy our legacy. Remember, love is not enough. We need to constantly build on that love with faith, trust, effort, wisdom, prayer, skill, and accountability.

Bio

When they met over 30 years ago, they were doing what they both love: serving God's people. What is now a fruitful, prosperous marriage ministry started long before The Franklins even said, "I do." Featured on TBN's Praise the Lord and radio appearances on Worldwide Core Radio, WHFR 89.3 and WNUC, Ministers Ron and LaShun Franklin have transformed couples' lives across the nation through their transparent, down-to-earth way of delivering God's Word—catapulting them into their God-given destiny.

After meeting and falling in love during their service in a community choir, they were appointed leaders over the youth ministry at their church. Because of their passion and unfailing love for children, they not only touched the hearts of little ones—they transformed whole families. By 2003, their compassion for couples, their commitment to the sanctity of marriage, and their desire to deliver ministry in truth and freedom, Songs of Solomon Marriage Ministries was birthed. Songs of Solomon provides married couples with marriage tune-ups, weekend retreats, resources and—more importantly—spiritual accountability partners for life.

While it may come natural for couples to treat marriage like a contract or business transaction, The Franklins' message is loud and clear: Marriage is a covenant. Through Biblical sound teaching, role playing and the 10-week course, Marriage Bootcamp, they were on a mission to serve notice to married couples—young and old—that divorce is not an option.

In 2016, the ministry evolved and took flight as they formed the Song of Solomon Relationship Institute, which serves individuals, couples, families and institutions world-wide in the arena of developing and maintaining healthy relationships. SOS has served over 1300 couples and countless others through their ministry and media presence.

As licensed ministers of the Gospel, certified marriage educators, and certified Biblical counselors, they're committed to traveling around the world to encourage couples to realize that their stumbling blocks are not a reason to head to divorce court. It's a reason to grow closer to God, using those bricks as building blocks to great marital success in the Kingdom.

For speaking engagements or more information, visit www.sofsri.com

ELEVEN

Unforgiveness: The Root

Kenneth & Adrienne Nears

Perfecting Marriage Ministries

Unforgiveness is holding on to past hurts that have been done to you by someone else. Bitterness is a result of that unforgiveness that permeates through the veins of our lives. Unforgiveness causes one to have a foothold on the past. This foothold will make it difficult in striving to move forward in your relationships.

Because God is love, it makes sense that unforgiveness is sin. It's like poison to our spiritual, mental, emotional, and physical body. Hebrews 12:15 reads, See to it that no bitter root springs up to cause trouble and defile many) (defiled meaning in the Greek; polluted or contaminated). Jesus said we must forgive from our hearts and that if we don't forgive, he will not forgive us. Matt 18:35.

Imagine coming into a new relationship. You are so in love with each other. Then everyday life sets in. You begin to see the challenges of being married and building your lives together. Agreements are difficult to achieve. Words are spewn that trigger feelings of past hurts. Silence becomes a new way of communication, because of the words hurled at you that were offensive.

When offended, we no longer look at our spouses with the same love and excitement we had from the beginning. Offenses break down communication with one another. Offense is caused by a negative emotion that is created by something being said or done that you didn't like. The relationship begins to breakdown, and we build a wall around ourselves for protection. There is no romance, no respect for one another, no connection, etc.

You may think what is this? Why am I feeling this way? Why has our relationship changed? Why do I not have any regard for how my spouse is feeling? We can't seem to resolve the simplest conflict. Have you thought that perhaps you are harboring some unforgiven offenses from the past, and maybe some present offenses?

Sometimes we are walking in unforgiveness and don't realize it. Symptoms of unforgiveness are anger, bitterness, inability to resolve conflicts, being mean, feeling insecure, being curt or sarcastic.

Consider Colossians 23:19 KJV (Husbands are not to be bitter with their wives but treat them with love and respect.

Wives don't put fuel in the fire. Deal with your husband in love and show kindness to him.

And let the wife see that she respects her husband. Ephesians 5:33 KJV.

Put a search light on yourself. The song says "Search me Lord. If you find anything that shouldn't be take it out and strengthen me".

A good example of unforgiveness is the story about the Sycamine/Sycamore Tree in Luke 17. God used the Sycamine Tree as an illustration when teaching the disciples about unforgiveness and bitterness. The Sycamine Tree is a beautiful tree that has long strong deep roots and bares a very bitter fruit. This tree can survive in any type of weather and grows best in dry areas. Even cutting it down at the base will not destroy the root of this tree. It is said that this tree could have roots up to 30 feet deep. Can you imagine how deep that is?

Unforgiveness and bitterness is much like the Sycamore Tree. We look so beautiful on the outside and appear to be so sweet. But if we have bitterness in our hearts. The fruit of the spirit are not exhibited in our lives. There is no gentleness, love, peace, kindness, joy, patience, and goodness. At this point we are in a dry place. Water is necessary for life. John 7:38 - He that believeth on me, as the scripture hath said, out of his belly shall flow rivers of living water. We need the rivers of water to flow in our lives in order to be free of unforgiveness and bitterness.

When dealing with unforgiveness and bitterness, we must get to the root of the offense. Unforgiveness and bitterness run deep into our soul when it is fed by the offenses that lie in our hearts. If we allow unforgiveness and bitterness to continue to grow in our hearts, they will steal our joy, peace and kill our spiritual life, leaving us unhappy, depressed and unfulfilled. We don't need a lot of faith in order to forgive. If we just have the faith of a grain of a mustard seed ("mustard" is the Greek word *sinapi*, which refers to the small mustard plant that grows from a tiny, miniscule seed), it is possible to forgive.

Forgive quickly, ask God to give you a heart of forgiveness. It is the will of God for us to live free and have joy that is everlasting. (Luke 17:1-6 KJV)

Forgiveness is essential. Matt 6:15, But if you do not forgive men of their trespasses, neither will your father forgive you. We want God to forgive us, so it is necessary for us to forgive others. Even though, it's a tough pill to swallow.

We have experienced offenses many times in our marriage. Some offenses have been very difficult and challenging to forgive. It's not as simple as "get over it". Our first marriages failed for many reasons. Our second marriages presented new challenges, as well. The expectations of what we thought our blended family should be, was not what it was turning out to be. There were a lot of outside interferences that caused resentment, bitterness and hurt. Not to mention, the offenses and hurt we had of our own. We dealt with a lot of baby mama drama. It was so hard to overcome some of those difficult situations. There were dark spaces in our marriage, and it took time for us to navigate through some of the problems we were facing. We had to seek God for guidance.

At the beginning of our marriage, we didn't realize that we ourselves were still broken and hadn't completely healed from the hurt, resentment and disappointments of our previous marriages. I (Adrienne) personally had to ask God for a heart of forgiveness.

Our children were hurting and acting out in the only way knew how. They were affected on so many different levels. There were many sleepless nights filled with tears. The feeling of anger, disappointment and resentment was present. I (Adrienne) was angry about being blamed for trying to do a good thing and nobody understood my efforts in trying to bring our family together, and a lot of other things. I (Kenneth) had feelings of disappointment and failure in being the husband and the man of the house. Like the sycamore tree, we looked beautiful on the outside. When we stepped out of the house, you would never know the anger and turmoil that we had going on in the inside.

During this season, I (Adrienne) was very anxious and overwhelmed. At times, I thought our marriage would not survive. Working through the forgiveness process was not an easy or comfortable task, but in order to have peace, it was necessary. I prayed and asked God to heal me and to give me the strength to forgive. There was a lot of disarray in the home. I asked myself, "How in the world were we going to get through this?"

As God lead me, I spoke with my children and asked them to forgive me for any pain that I may have caused them. I asked God to forgive me for not acknowledging him in all my ways. Parts of this forgiveness journey was together with my husband, but parts of it was alone with just me and God.

We fasted and sought wise counsel. Seeking help and journaling was my saving grace. We asked each other for forgiveness and took responsibility for whatever part we played in causing the offenses. It was necessary to immerse ourselves into God's word and read about forgiveness in books to gain a clear knowledge about unforgiveness and how to forgive. Offering forgiveness is not an easy task and continues in our journey, today.

Sometimes, I still shake my head at the awesomeness of God. We are still a work in progress after 32 years. I have still been hurt and offended, but God has continued to rescue my heart and through my love and faith in him He has kept my heart tender.

In marriage, we will often offend each other. It doesn't matter where you come from, what language you speak, at some time or another you will offend, not intentionally, but it does happen.

Remember to

- Acknowledge your part and ask forgiveness
- Pray and fast when prompted by Holy Spirit
- Read scriptures on forgiveness
- Seek wise counsel
- Journal to process your emotions
- Remember the good things about your relationship

With the love that we have for God and for one another and an open heart to hear the voice of God, we are doing well. We realize that unforgiveness is a destroyer of life. We want to live a free and abundant life in God. And we want for God to receive the glory out of our lives and marriages.

Check your emotions. Examine your thoughts. Ask yourself these questions. Who do you need to forgive? What did they do to you that needs forgiving? How has this affected you overall? Once you have done this and have asked God to forgive you.

Then seek forgiveness and work on freeing yourself from the bondage of unforgiveness.

Our prayer for anyone reading this chapter is that you don't have to live a life captive to unforgiveness. In everyday life you will be offended, someone will hurt you. Forgive them. Don't be afraid or ashamed to seek godly counsel. Always examine yourself and your thoughts so you can forgive quickly. God wants us to be free of offenses. He who the Son sets free is free indeed. John 8:36 (KJV)

Bio

Pastors Kenneth and Adrienne Nears got involved in marriage ministry over 15 years ago. During this time, God gave them a special passion for marriages and along with that came a passion to help men and women become whole and well-rounded, in their relationships, especially blended families. They believe a strong marriage means strong healthy families, communities, and churches. After attending many seminars and events and becoming leaders of various church marriage ministries, they were led to move beyond the boundaries of the church and form a marriage ministry/coaching service without walls, "Perfecting Love Marriage Ministries".

Kenneth and Adrienne have been married 32 years. They are a blended family of 8 children and 15 grand children. Being a blended family themselves, they totally understand the ups and downs that come along with being a blended a family. Blending families is definitely a challenge. There haven't been many situations that Kenneth and Adrienne haven't encountered. As a result, they have a special passion for blended families.

With the knowledge they have gained, they are able to give tools and encouragement to many couples that need guidance. They do this by holding seminars, coaching, and providing marriage building activities. Perfecting Love Marriage Ministries also reaches out to single and engaged couples who desire to be married.

Their personal goal is that every marriage be strong and successful, and God be glorified in relationships.

Contact: Perfecting Love Marriage Ministry

Email: perfectingluv@gmail.com

IG: Perfectingluv

Facebook: Perfecting Love Empowerment Services

TWELVE

Yours, Mines, & Ours: Chronicles of a Blended Family

Byron & Gwendolyn Holloway

Holding Hands Marriage Ministry

Merriam-Webster defines the word **blend** as a verb, its meaning is to mix by thoroughly intermingling different varieties or grades together. To intimately or unobtrusively combine two separates into an integrated whole, therefore producing a harmonious effect. To merge with another so that one is not clearly distinguishable from the other. Similar in behavior, appearance or mannerism.

When using the term '**blended family**' it signifies that either one or both parents have children from a previous relationship;

but have since married or remarried and combined to form a new life together. This newly formed family will often face a series of challenges and compromises as they grow on this journey. All the parties involved must work together to figure out their different roles and responsibilities within the family unit.

It's vitally important that both the husband and the wife form a united front in helping the family develop and be productive, as God intended. While the parents are becoming one in matrimony, they must also be aware of the uncertainty that the children will face adjusting to a new parent and new siblings. This realistic goal of blending will become more evident as the family makes prayer a priority (Mat 6:33 KJV).

When describing a blended family, people frequently refer to them using the word **stepparent or stepchildren,** a term which can have negative connotations or deem as less valuable. Keep in mind, the only steps, should be the ones leading to the front door. The added family member(s) will struggle enough, requiring guidance, lots of love and the ability to make mistakes without harsh consequences and titles that discourage their worth.

In our home, we prefer the phrase **bonus children,** like having an extra gift (Psalm 127:3 KJV) Each child is given the grace to be an individual yet still settle into their new life, as an important part of a bigger family.

As everyone gets to know each other, don't expect to see immediate changes over night, the hope is to cultivate lasting and trusting relationships, with a mutual respect, that lasts forever.

Think of it like this: When making a peanut butter and jelly sandwich, each ingredient is very tasty by itself; however, when you combine the two together on your favorite bread, the results are amazing. And while being amazing should be one of the characteristics of a blended family, you must work at intentionally making it happen or at the end of the day you're left with a messy sandwich, dripping everywhere, that no one wants.

Our story began March 19, 2005, the day we were married. I (Gwendolyn) came to the marriage with two children ages 17 and 10 years old and my husband's three children were 15, 8 and 5 years old.

Our children were not strangers, we had worshipped in the same church for several years, so they were acquainted with each other. When we decided to get married, we never asked our children how they felt about the union, nor did we consult with them about living together. We both just assumed because they had gotten to know each other that everyone would just get along.

We were so excited about our love for one another, and we wanted to share our lives, all of us together, as one big happy family. We were so not prepared for the challenges, the demands and the lack of cooperation from the children. We overlooked the warning signs, the involvement of the other parents, the brokenness and resentment from the children.

We had little direction for guiding our newly blended family. We had no manual or toolbox full of instructions for perfectly blending our family together. We just made up the rules as we went along, instead of having a well thought-out and prayed out vision (Prov 29:18 KJV).

In our new home, we had two children who lived with us permanently, (the eldest one was preparing to leave for college in less than 1 year), two children who came every other weekend and one who got so out of line, that the decision was made for him to stay with his mom.

Once we shifted into the house together, it was important to us that each child had their own space. We encouraged them to bring things from their other house, to make this home feel comfortable to them. We purchased new furniture and allowed then to decorate their own rooms. However even with our best intentions, we were often challenged with disrespectful behavior from a few of the children. We were so busy making the schedule work, pick up's, drop off's, different schools, visitations and still getting used to being a newly married couple. Sometimes the children would pit my husband and I against each other, asking both of us for favors, yet being discreet enough to ask separately. The children were testing our loyalty to one another, and this caused irritation early in the marriage. We were so unprepared, charting this new territory.

We learned that the younger kids were unhappy and still grieving and longing for restoration to their prior lives with both original parents. There was crying, tantrums and outbursts. Children have a way of trying to manipulate their parents to get what they want, sometimes it worked and sometimes it was met with discipline (Prov 23:13-14 MSG).

We tried having family meetings. Most often, it was just the adults talking and the children would go silent. This caused even more of a strain as we tried to move forward as a family.

My wife and I both worked outside the home. We made good wages and paid our fair share of child support. We took the kids places and tried doing fun things that they enjoyed, while waiting for the glue to meld us together. The constant driving force in our life during this time, was our love for one another and our faith in Jesus Christ. Both of us were strong prayer warriors and felt that we were in tune with the Holy Spirit (Eph 6:10 KJV).

Another challenging factor during our early years of marriage, was that my husband acknowledged and accepted his call to start a ministry. (1 Timothy 3:4-5 AMP) Excited as we were for what God had shown him, all of our lives were going to drastically change again.

As the years progressed, we expected our children to become a part of the ministry when they were home. We tried grooming them and developing giftings in them as drummers, dancers, and youth leaders, but this didn't always work.

When the eldest one went away to college, the other three began to have their own interests. The weekend visits slowly turned into once-a-month visits.

Our children exhibited growing pains, disobedience, involvement with marijuana, shouting matches, running away from home and blatant disrespect! (Prov 3:1-2 KJV). We stepped in as support when one child was arrested. We were frequently called on for financial assistance. Once again, it was only prayer that got us through those rough times (1 Thess 5:17 KJV).

Over the years, we have stood on the word of God concerning our children and we await the manifestation of Acts 2:39 KJV, "For the promise is unto you, and to your children, and to all that are afar off, even as many as the Lord, our God, shall call."

Our oldest child will turn 35 this year, she's independent, checks on us daily and serves the Lord. Our second eldest child is 34 years old, he's a sweetheart, a hard worker and has matured a lot over the years. He is our "Prodigal Son." He also makes himself available every time we need him. Sad to say, our other 3 children are estranged from us (because of their own choice) they've rejected our love and the lifestyle that we have chosen to live. However, just as Christ has given us grace, we offer that same grace and forgiveness to them. We both diligently cover them and our grandchildren in prayer, calling out their names and declaring what the word of God says concerning their life (Phil 4:6 KJV).

Looking back, would we do things differently? Yes! No one is perfect. We thank God for His mercy.

So although there have been challenging times with our children (birthdays, Christmas, Mothers and Father's day) not celebrating with all of them together, we still wish them well and are believing God to restore that which has been broken. We know that faith, mercy, and love are primary ingredients to the rebuilding of the blend.

Here are a few suggestions that may nurture a more successful blend:

1. Seek out Christian Family Counseling.

2. Set weekly Family meetings.

3. As the parent, spend more personal time with the other's children.

4. Communicate often and openly.

5. Let all the kids know how much you love them.

6. Let the biological parent be primarily responsible for discipline.

7. Set rules and boundaries in the beginning.

8. Treat each child as an individual, do not draw comparisons.

9. Don't force the blend, give each individual time to adjust.

10. Insist on mutual respect.

11. Include them in daily prayer.

12. Never allow the children to divide the marriage.

Bio

Pastor Byron Holloway received the gift of the Holy ghost, by water baptism, under the leadership of Bishop Tom H. Watson, of Gloryland Apostolic Cathedral, in Richmond, Ca. He went on to fulfill many appointments in the church, in preparation for God's calling. He was a faithful teacher and held the position as a member of the Board of Trustees. Pastor Byron acknowledged his call to preach and teach the Gospel of Jesus Christ on June 17, 1997.

Lady Gwendolyn began her walk with the Lord in August 1992, at New Bethel Apostolic Church of San Francisco, Ca. She immediately began working in the children's ministry, teaching and leading young people to the Lord. Over the years, Lady Gwendolyn has been instrumental in leadership, administration, the music ministry and developing other departments, in preparation for servitude. She has the heart of a worshipper and is adamant about teaching others to pray.

In 2006, after hearing the voice of the Lord, Pastor Byron was obedient, and Living Bread Ministry was birthed. The church developed a feeding program, with a full pantry for those in need, they started a yearly coat drive, a tutoring program for after school neighborhood children and partnered with an overseas ministry, supplying shoes and books.

After many years of servitude and due diligence, the Lord shifted the ministry, now known as "New Beginning Worship Center," Pastor's Byron and Gwendolyn Holloway quickly got to work, putting their hands to the plow, teaching, re-building, supporting and being an example for others, to live a life pleasing unto Christ.

Pastor Byron and Gwendolyn Holloway are the founders of Holding Hands Marriage Ministries in Vallejo Ca. where they counsel married and engaged couples on the biblical principles of operating as one in God.

Lady Gwendolyn has led "The Women of Grace and Purpose Ministry" operating as a theatrical biblical production, where the women of the Bible come alive through plays and skits.

Pastor Byron's latest endeavor has been to author his first book titled "Digging My Way Out". This book has an instructor's manual and a student edition, for those who want to have " An in-depth Study of the Word of God".

Pastor Byron and Gwendolyn Holloway have been married 17 years. They are a blended family and share 5 adult children and 4 grandchildren. They live in Vallejo, California

Contact: Holding Hands Marriage Ministry

Email: 2holdinghandsmarriageministry@gmail.com

Facebook: Holding Hands Marriage Ministry

Marriage Helps

A Couple's Prayer

Dear Father, thank you for loving us so graciously. Our words and actions have not lined up with your word. Forgive us for acting in the flesh. We invite you into our marriage. We recognize that we desperately need your help. We know that you are able to keep us. Heal us from the wounds we have inflicted on one another. Help us to walk in humility and to love each other like you love us. Show us where we need to grow and teach us how to not be easily angered or frustrated. Remind us both to offer each other loads of grace when we need it most. In Jesus' name we pray.

Amen.

Scriptures for Encouragement

He heals the brokenhearted And binds up their wounds. Psalm 147:3

Jesus said to him, "If you can believe, all things are possible to him who believes." Mark 9:23 NKJV

He sent His word and healed them, And delivered *them* from their destructions. Psalm 107:20

Casting all your care upon Him, for He cares for you. I Peter 5:7

But He said, "The things which are impossible with men are possible with God." Luke 18:27

The king's heart *is* in the hand of the LORD, *Like* the rivers of water; He turns it wherever He wishes. Prov 21:1

Be joyful in hope, patient in affliction, faithful in prayer. Romans 12:12 NIV

Fear not, for I *am* with you; Be not dismayed, for I *am* your God. I will strengthen you, Yes, I will help you, I will uphold you with My righteous right hand.' Isaiah 41:10

www.ingramcontent.com/pod-product-compliance
Lightning Source LLC
Chambersburg PA
CBHW060823190426
43197CB00038B/2202